Cat R

Rescuing s
streets of London

by Nichola Kirk

*Many human names and details have been changed to protect identities, but the cat names are all correct

Contents

Introduction 4
Linford 18
Tortie and the Pick-Up Truck 23
Felix and the nine ferals 34
Daisy in the Shoebox 50
Casper and the string 58
Bob in Central London 64
The Bracelet 66
Paddy 70
The Fox at Piccadilly Circus 73
Rosie and the Adventure Playground 78
A nice surprise 85
Yin Yang 87
Teamwork 89
Cemetery 1 90
Tintin 96
Terry 100
Catflap 109
Rescuing Tails 113
The Mad Cat Gentleman 117
Windsor The Second 123
A Mad Cat Lady 138
The Persians 158
Cemetery 2 168
In the end 174
Epilogue 186

This book is dedicated to all those who spend their time, whether paid or in your spare time, to helping those in need. Whether you help a family member, volunteer for a charity, feed garden wildlife, look after a stray cat or adopt a pet.
However you help out, thank you.

Introduction

This is the story of my time working as an Animal Rescuer, rescuing cats (and the odd dog and fox too) for a Charity called the Celia Hammond Animal Trust (aka C.H.A.T) in East London. It was truly a life-changing experience, a dream come true. Yet they were also the hardest few years of my life, both physically and emotionally. Feel free to skip ahead to the cat stories themselves, then you can pop back here for a bit of background whenever you are ready. Thank you for reading our story (mine, the charity's and the cat's).

Not many people have had the opportunity to be as deeply immersed in the cat welfare crisis as I was and therefore can be aware of the sheer quantity of unwanted kittens born every year. It is impossible to describe the extent of the issue, or to imagine it, even when you are told that there are over one million stray cats on the streets of London alone. It is hard to believe because stray cats tend to come out at night, live in back gardens, and travel constantly so that they are barely visible to most of us.

I joined the charity in July 2010 not really knowing much about cats and not having that much experience with them, apart from a weekly socialising session at a cat shelter in West Yorkshire and a bit of voluntary home-checking. Cats had not been one of my favourite animals. However, a couple of days with the rescued cats at the charity, sitting with a mother cat curled and purring in my lap while her little ones played around me soon changed that.

The founder of the charity, and my direct line manager, Celia Hammond, had been a famous model in the 1960s. She became drawn into animal welfare when she was taken to see how fur was produced for clothing and immediately after refused to model anything made from fur. She encouraged other models to get on board too until her influence helped make fur very unfashionable. She became a dedicated animal rights activist and eventually got involved in the rescue of her favourite animal. Over the years she filled her own home so full of rescue cats that she decided to expand it, turning it into a Sanctuary. Once this was full too, realising that you cannot take in every cat, she started to promote neutering. She opened two rescue and neuter clinics in London, where cat overpopulation has always been worst. She has an incredible drive and is still heavily involved in the running of the charity when, as she says she could have 'retired to knit by the fire'. (Although I later found out that she does not like knitting.) She used to have long blond hair just like mine, and though it is still straight, it has now turned grey. She has never minded, she has more important things to worry about.

Working at C.H.A.T was one of the few jobs I have had where being only five foot did not make me feel short, as coincidentally many of my colleagues were too, although still taller than me. I would tie up my hair in a ponytail to keep it out the way so I was already ready for a rescue. I learned quickly that it was better to tie it up than having it trail in the muck when I was searching under cars for missing cats or sheds for missing kittens. I usually wore jeans to protect my legs from prickly hedges along with the C.H.A.T navy-blue fleece.

The charity would never put a healthy cat to sleep. In fact, it would not put *any* cat to sleep unless it had no chance of survival. Hundreds of hours were spent fixing broken bones, giving physiotherapy to semi-paralysed cats, picking fleas off flea-anaemic kittens, or finding the right home for kittens with Cerebellar Hypoplasia. I sometimes wondered if we would have had a better chance against the overpopulation crisis if we had not been so determinedly opposed to putting to sleep some of these cats to sleep. But then I think about Linford, and Paddy, Tintin and Casper, and all of my favourite Corona infected kittens. I know that even now, I would make just the same effort to save them and look back in respect and admiration at the charity who fought to save them despite the odds against them.

As a cat lover, you would be amazed at how common it is for cats to be left behind. The number of calls that the charity got about this was extreme. When the charity was made aware of a friendly stray, we would assume that it had either been kicked out of its home or had been left behind by its' owners after they moved. For those that came into the clinic, we would keep our fingers crossed that they may have simply gotten lost after chasing a mate too far and that an owner would come for them soon, but they rarely did. I cannot understand why people get a cat if they cannot provide a home for the rest of its life. The number of calls the charity took from people wanting to give up a cat showed that 'moving home' was the most common reason for giving up a cat.

The recession certainly seemed to make this worse when people were forced to downsize or move into cheaper rented accommodation and not be allowed to take their pets. I could understand in these circumstances as the family could not have planned or prepared for recession. However, in *other* circumstances, I wished they had thought ahead the twenty years that a cat might live before taking on the responsibility in the first place. I also wished that more landlords would allow well-behaved, neutered pets. This would make a significant difference to the numbers of cats being abandoned. I had hopes of instigating a campaign to try to make landlords more lenient of these sorts of things, but after some research into it, it was far too big a campaign for such a small charity to take on and difficult to get the larger charities interested.

I always felt that it was important for the animal charities to work together and I was confused about why they did not do so already. I tried many times to get different rescue organisations to collaborate on various issues, we were all working for animal welfare after all. But we could never agree on the details, such as which individuals should be caught and how they should be caught, and what should happen to them once caught, so struggled to work effectively together. Even I disagreed with Celia's insistence on rehoming so many that could have easily be returned neutered, but it was not something I could argue against, as she was right that we should do whatever we can to give the best life possible to those that had come into our care.

Since I was twelve years old, all I had wanted to do was to be an RSPCA Inspector. It was a respectable, active job. It was very hands-on, helping both animals and people, with a huge variety of work. It seemed to fit me perfectly. At the time you had to be twenty-two to apply, so I stayed on at school to get my A-levels, and then went to University to get a degree, in the hope that it might just increase my chances of competing. After university, I applied for the job excitedly and with full expectation of getting an interview. But, despite ten years of effort, I did not have enough professional animal handling experience for them. Unfazed, my next mission was to resolve this. I volunteered with animals for two different charities at least twice a week, around an office job. I then found the job offer at C.H.A.T. Celia Hammond interviewed me. She had her phone pressed to her ear, while on hold to the police about a cat. I never found out what that was about. I would start to answer her questions and then she would start talking on the phone. Between calls she asked me questions again that I had tried to answer twice, but then the phone rang again. I gave my answers instead to 'Si the Catman', and Naomi, Celia's 'right-hand' woman. They suggested that some receptionist work may be required as necessary. I was used to this sort of work, but often worried about my squeaky voice on the phone. I did not mention this. I also neglected to mention that there was a possibility that I was allergic to cats. I had tested it out when volunteering with cats and it seemed to only be mild. An antihistamine a day would sort me out.

After the interview, I reported back to my family that it seemed like an excessively stressful job. When they offered me the job, I consciously chose to accept the difficulties, and reminded myself and my family of that fact frequently over the next few years, to justify the pressure I put myself under. I had decided I could handle it, and although it might be very difficult, I thought it was only a temporary stepping-stone to my dream career at the RSPCA.

However, the next time that I filled out the RSPCA application form, it had changed. They had added the question, 'Would you be able to put a healthy animal to sleep?'

I had thought about it before, and I knew already that I would be able to put a sick, dying animal to sleep. I would be upset about it, but I would know it was for the best and I could give the animal a cuddle as it went to sleep to be safe from further pain and suffering forever.

But could I put a healthy animal to sleep?

I understood that the RSPCA had to do this. To be able to stop the suffering of other animals, they had to make room by putting to sleep some of the animals that were difficult to rehome. But could I do it personally? Perhaps if the animal was in a slaughterhouse and was about to be killed anyway?

Perhaps if there was an aggressive dog that had attacked a child?

No.

Even in these situations, I could not be the one to do it while watching the life fade away. They would not be going to a better place because they were not suffering here and now. I decided that I no longer wanted to work for the RSPCA. I realised that C.H.A.T were absolutely incredible for refusing to put healthy animals to sleep, despite the stresses that caused. Realising this was the beginning of my realisation that rescue at C.H.A.T *was* my dream job.

After my first year, I discovered that Celia had initially been disappointed that I did not know how to scruff a cat when I first started. So I learnt quickly. I was very rarely hurt by a scruffed cat and those few times had almost always been my own fault. They happened when I had used my other arm to tuck under a cat's back legs to support their weight as I lifted them, and they managed to get their claws into my arm. The time that hurt the most was a little black female, barely more than a kitten. She had been born in a working garage to a stray mother. She had somehow managed to twist herself within her own skin and sink her teeth into my arm. I can only assume that I did not have enough of her scruff in my hand as I have never known another cat to be able to do this. I still have the scars so will always remember her. I proudly tell the story often, as despite having her teeth deep in my arm, I still managed to lift her gently and secure her in a carrier.

I dragged information out of anyone who knew anything to find out as much as I could about the equipment, trapping methods, and Celia's specific trapping rules. I insisted on being taken out to watch and gain experience as often as possible, even getting up with Si at 5am when that was the only option to start my training. It very quickly became so much more than a job. It was a way of life. My colleagues became as close as family. We would laugh all day, and cry in each other's arms when our favourite animals passed on. I could not have done the job without their support. Celia soon accepted that I could do the job, sending me on increasingly complex rescues. I have since been told that she eventually found me invaluable and really respected my opinions. I had immersed myself completely in the charity, to the point that my partner and family would worry and ask if I was working too much and if I should slow down a bit. But how could I? I was needed. I was making a difference.

Each morning, I would look through the rescue book, which we called the Problem Book and prioritise which animals could come into the shelter and which could not. This was a horrible task, particularly as the shelter never actually had a cage spare to put a new arrival into. It had to be managed very closely and carefully with new cats coming in as others were being rehomed. I wanted to ensure that only the cats that truly needed us that would be better off, not worse, would be the ones to come to us.

The emotional torment for me of knowing that a litter of kittens could not come into the shelter because another person had decided to bring their pet in for adoption with an excuse such as, 'I don't have time for it anymore' was unbearable. It was impossible to explain to the person bringing the cat in what consequences their actions would have. They often stated that they were doing the cat a favour by giving it over to someone who would have more time for it. But they were splitting it up from the family it probably loved, to live in a cage, possibly for as long as a year, then to be rehomed to strangers in a strange environment. Whereas for a cat that has been living stray, abandoned or feral, a rescue centre must seem like heaven.

Cat Rescuer

I had refused many callers who had asked us to take a cat in because they were moving, simply because there was no room anywhere in the charity, but there was always the fear that it would be so easy for them to just dump the poor cat somewhere. Like in a skip, or a river, or by the three-lane A13. These are all places where I have picked up more than one dumped cat in the past. I have picked up very many cats left behind by owners who have moved away, convincing themselves that cats can fend for themselves. They really cannot, they might catch the occasional mouse or find some scraps, but it is not enough to keep them healthy.

Many calls to the charity seem to assume that it would take their cats. Even if the caller did not really have a reason for not wanting them anymore. One excuse we heard a few times was that they were too expensive to feed. When asked what they were feeding them, they would respond with a luxurious cat food. We pointed out that they would be forced to eat whatever food was donated at the charity, so to try a cheaper food at home first before giving up on them.

Some wanted to give up their cat due to a newborn baby. I do empathise with people in these situations, but I wish they would do their research before they choose to give up their family pet. Being pregnant does result in a fear of toxoplasmosis infection. The health professionals do not help, sometimes even recommending that cats are rehomed. You would have to eat an infected cat's excrement to get toxoplasmosis, so simply wearing gloves when cleaning the litter tray would protect mother and baby. I have always thought that it is good for kids to grow up with cats. They learn that if they are not gentle, the cat runs out of their way, and they (hopefully) get reprimanded by their parents, so they learn a great skill. I also like it because it raises a whole new generation of cat lovers, of course.

Pet shops are not safe places to give kittens to. The pet shop owners themselves are often reasonable people. But they make a profit out of selling the animals, and so are much less vigilant than rescue centres about where the animals are going to. Some want to breed them, putting them through endless pregnancies for a bit of profit. Some buy a kitten on a whim because it is cute, only to realise very soon after that kittens are actually hard work. I wish people would take them to the same pet shop where they bought them, leaving them on the doorstep or in the shop in their carrier if the pet shop refuses to accept them back, like people have done at the clinic. I think that if everyone who changed their mind about a kitten that they had purchased were to take it back, even if years later, it would not be long before pet shops were as overwhelmed as the rescue centres and would be forced to be responsible about who they sold their pets to in the first place.

Oddly, most cats that end up in rescue centres are less than two years old. Perhaps this could be because people have not thought further than one or two years ahead when they get a pet. A year or two year, or even a lifetime 'guarantee' should be legally enforceable, where any person or place that sells an animal must guarantee to take it back on if the new owner changes their mind. All rescue centres that I know of already offer this for the whole life of the animal.

After a year of working at the charity, I realised that I was working excessively long hours and, although voluntary, it was putting a huge strain on me. Also, my diet whilst working at C.H.A.T could certainly not be considered healthy so I promised myself to make more time for a proper lunch, not just survive on takeaway. I kept denying that I was stressed to my partner and my family, but they could see the effect it was having better than I could. I insisted that I wanted to stay at the charity as I was certain that I could make a huge difference to the running of the rescue side of the clinic. I would not give up until I had achieved this. At one stage I had to take a break due to dizzy spells that were apparently caused by anxiety. But I did not feel anxious, I felt determined. Me and my partner decided to buy our own house outside of London, to give me a break at weekends and Celia agreed to let me work condensed hours to enable this whilst not reducing my effectiveness at the charity.

Though it was not long before my desire to help the charity get organised to be capable of having an even bigger impact on the stray cat world took back over me.

I threw myself even more into it, trying to rescue as much as possible. I wanted to pick up every pregnant cat and every litter of kittens that we were contacted about. I was told it was not possible, but I did not want to believe it.

I took on managing the charity's volunteers as well, to make sure they always had enough in to feed and clean the cats, so that I would never have to, giving me more time to get out and rescue them.

Then I took on managing the fosterers from the rehoming officers, so that I could make sure that we had as many as possible, letting me bring in even more litters of kittens.

Of course, I eventually wore myself out again, but until then, I was sure I was beginning to make a difference.

The clinic at the time was in the process of being extended slightly for the rescue side of the charity. I wanted to formulate a plan to make maximum use of it, rather than just carrying on as we were. I wanted Celia to see why we needed such a plan from my point of view as we had disagreed about it. Every time we brought in a cat to be neutered with the agreement that it would go back to where it was fed and had shelter, and a person to tell us if it needed to see a vet, Celia would want to rehome it to a cosy fireside life instead. I thought she was being unfair to all the other cats that needed us. Perhaps I was being harsh. It is hard to tell when opinion and emotion are all tangled up in it. Celia had stopped reading the problem book a long time ago, because I had taken it over and she trusted us to ensure the urgent jobs were dealt with. But it also meant that she was not seeing how very many cats desperately needed our help. To me, every cat she chose to rehome was another neuter-return that could not come in for another month or two, that might have kittens in the meantime. Or another cat from a genuinely bad situation that would lose out on the chance of a better home. I needed to figure out a way to show her how bad it was. The charity had never quantified it before. Maybe because they were afraid to see the numbers, knowing for sure how impossible it all was. It was very difficult to explain my reasoning for my decisions without the facts and figures.

At the time, we prioritised injured cats, cats in dangerous places or situations, pregnant strays, and mother cats with kittens born outdoors. By August, the height of kitten season, we got up to four calls a *day* about litters of kittens born in sheds all over East and North London. Even the kitten intake had to be ranked again by which litters were most at risk. In one summer, I found litters that had been born in washing machines, toolboxes, under tarpaulin covered barbeques, and even on a front doorstep.

Neuter-returns were carried out whenever there was enough time and space for both us rescuers to bring them in, and the vets to look after them. Before bringing in new neuter-returns, I would return all those from the previous week. First we made absolutely sure that they were sufficiently healed to go back outside. Celia would personally double-check every single one.

To achieve my aim of getting some facts to show how dire… or achievable… the overpopulation situation was, I spent every spare minute counting the number of calls we had taken in the Problem Book for the whole year, and then the previous year too.

I noticed trends in types of calls throughout the year, which would help us to prepare better for future months. For example, mum and kitten calls were worst in August, with a clear trend line decreasing into winter.

The year of 2012 certainly had been a worse year than 2011. I suspected that perhaps the weather in the winter of 2011 had led to the problems in 2012, when very cold weather never really came, and so stray cats carried on breeding past Autumn. The recession may also have had an effect of course. Whatever the reason, I was glad to have the evidence to show Celia that it was not always so bad, and we could manage this year, if only we were a little more organised, decisive and collaborative.

My summary of 2012 was ready in time for a meeting I arranged to request that we make a plan for the year 2013.

We started by agreeing the priorities of the types of calls into high, medium and low.

We agreed that the high priority cats would always be brought in for rehoming. These were still the injured or ill strays, the pregnant cats, and any whose lives were in danger. The number of these alone would be 655 for the year. This did not take into account the number that would be dumped on the doorstep or brought in without warning. We expected to home around 900 in a year so could handle this… but any more? We were not going to be able to help them directly and we could not carry on as we were, letting the situations worsen and responding only to emergencies, we needed to get ahead.

To deal with the low priority calls, we decided to put advice pages on the website to which we could refer people, so they would at least have some advice on the next steps, rather than just being left with no knowledge of the best way to help themselves. These were the people who had a new baby in the house, were allergic to their cats, whose cat was urinating inside the house, attacking them, or falling out with their other pets. These came to 575 calls for the year.

The biggest problem was the mum and kittens. I had counted the number of calls, not the number of cats, because we did not know how big the litters were. There were 251 *litters* of owned kittens and 354 *litters* of stray kittens in 2012.

How could we possibly cope with this number? We certainly did not have the capacity to rehome even a decent proportion of these (maximum homes for up to 245 out of a likely 3025 cats). When I revealed the number, the room went silent, some sat with their heads in their hands. No wonder they had never wanted to see the figures before.

But we had to try.

If we failed to act more effectively, the crisis would never end. Those unneutered stray females would keep breeding. Cats Protection worked out that one female cat is able to produce 21,000 descendants in seven years.

My own calculation is based one cat usually having two litters a year, with an average of four kittens. If half of those are female, the following year, there would be five breeding females. Each would be likely to have two litters of four kittens. Therefore, in the second year, there would already be twenty breeding females, and all the males too. Imagine having to care for that many cats in your own home.

The charity came up with a plan to attempt to neuter the mothers of every litter, at the very least.

We would insist that owners have their cat neutered in return for our help rehoming the kittens. They would hold onto the kittens until they were eight weeks old, or the charity had room, effectively acting as a foster home.

We also agreed that we would do our very best to neuter and return all the mother cats living as strays, who had a reliable feeder and shelter. And we would have to decide whether to neuter and return or rehome the kittens of these strays on a case by case basis.

The plan meant that we could respond to every call in some way, and we were all on the same page about what needed to be done.

To carry it out, we would need more neuter and return space. Celia agreed to speed up the conversion of the new building, and to look into getting another rescue worker and neutering vet.

Entering the New Year with an action plan made me feel much better and more organised. I started to put the plan into action. I was so proud of the charity, and myself, and confident that, if we stuck to the plan, then the next year would be better.

Linford

An emergency call had come in which a cat had been hit by a car next to West Ham Football Club's ground and appeared badly hurt. The RSPCA had also been called, but they had not been sure when they would be able to send someone. The cat was bleeding so we were called too, to see if we could attend more quickly. I said I would go immediately. I was the only rescue worker in the office and with RTAs (Road Traffic Accidents) it was safest to have two people present to approach the injured cat from different sides in case it tried to run. Louise, one of the Animal Care Workers, agreed to come. She could scruff a cat quickly if necessary, so I was grateful to have her with me.

It was clear where we would find the cat as we pulled into the stadium's car park. A crowd had gathered around it. A frightened-looking black and white cat was huddled behind a very small bush in the middle of an open stretch of grass, trying and failing, to hide itself from the onlookers.

I jumped out of the van and as I grabbed a carrier, a woman in the crowd shouted, 'They're here. I'll get him.'

The woman from the crowd then started *running* towards the cat. Now, if you have ever tried to run towards a cat for any reason, you will know that they will run away. This poor cat was terrified already and was likely in a lot of pain, and surely not feeling very sociable.

Of course, before she even got close, and before I had time to react, the cat jumped up and ran away from her on three legs, dragging a back leg behind it. She continued to chase after it.

Did she think she could catch a cat? Did not she know that cats are *really* fast?

I surprised even myself, deciding in the moment that now was not a time for shyness or even politeness as I yelled at the top of my lungs, 'Stop!'

She stopped.

The cat stopped ahead of her on the open grass.

She turned to me and said, 'I'm trying to catch him for you.'

Trying to be both forceful and friendly in my tone, a difficult combination to manage, I replied, 'Thank you for your help, but I am afraid that you are not going to catch him that way.'

She looked surprised. I continued, 'Please back slowly away and let us do this our way.'

The crowd could see that I was right. I tried to explain that no cat can be caught by being chased, not even this injured one. They are too quick, too agile and much too clever. Even if they have just been hit by a car, apparently.

The gathered crowd joined me saying,

'Come back this way',

'Leave it alone now',

'Let them do it their way,' helping me to encourage the woman back to the pavement.

Once she was all the way back, far enough away from the cat to let it settle back down, crouching nervously in the open grass, I explained to her that we were trained to catch the cat causing it as little further injury and fright as possible and had methods and equipment to enable that. She agreed to let me take over.

I grabbed a carrier and my bag from the van. The bag had all sorts of random things in there and it went everywhere with me. It had my bright red diary, with all my notes about where I should be and when, a torch, charity leaflets, cable ties, snacks and water for me in case I was on a job where I was unable to get lunch and most importantly lots of different types of cat foods – tins of meat, pouches of kitten food, and a tray of fresh chicken. Crouching as low as I could to seem un-threatening, I held a strip of the chicken out ahead of me. I moved very slowly towards the cat. Pausing every time it looked like the cat might run, I managed to get close. I took my time so much that by the time I got within five feet of it, most of the crowd had dispersed, getting on with their day. My intention was to see how close I could get, if not close enough to touch it, and then put the trap there, with food inside to catch it that way.

But the cat was still too freaked out. All of a sudden, without even a twitch of warning first, he turned, ran and jumped through a hole in a fence at the edge of the carpark. The fence ran along the brick side of the football stadium, with a gap of only a foot between them. He crouched down in the gap, knowing I could not now get to him easily. I pushed the basket under the hole and covered it with a sheet, blocking him from coming back out that way without going into the basket. I hoped the basket looked a dark, cosy safe space that he might even choose to go into, if I could encourage him back towards it.

While I was looking for a way to get over the fence, an RSPCA van pulled up.

I explained my plan to him and described what we had seen of the poor cats' injuries so far - the blood and the limp.

The RSPCA inspector was much taller than me, and offered to help by climbing the fence to encourage the cat towards the basket. But the cat was not falling for it. Instead of going back towards the basket, it ran right past him, too fast to catch despite only using three legs. Further down the fenced in section, it found another hole and ran back out into the carpark, bolting past me and Louise, and stopped under the nearest car, an expensive looking, dark blue BMW.

I tried to reach him, but he was too far under. He had positioned himself perfectly in the middle and had plenty of options of directions to run to get away from me. The

RSPCA officer passed me his keys through the fence and asked me to get his dog catching rod. He did not want to jump back over the fence in case his landing scared the cat. I had never heard if dog catching rods could be used on cats, and was anxious, but he assured me it was safe. He gave me a quick lesson in using it, it was pretty simple, pull this bit to lengthen it, then pull that bit to tighten it. I never would have used it if I thought there was any other option for getting the cat to the vet before he hurt himself any further. Or if I had known that Celia had once seen a cat break its own neck struggling to get out of one. But I could not think of a better way at the time.

I laid on the floor by the BMW, inching the pole towards the cat. He did not move. I managed to rest the loop over his head. He still did not move, he lay still, tense, watching me with wide, yellow eyes. I used the mechanism to pull the loop into a snug collar around his neck. Still, he did not react. I started to tug him gently towards me, he pulled back at first, and then twisted a little but mostly just let me pull him. Maybe he was all out of energy. Once I got him to the edge of the car though, he started to freak out. I moved fast, scruffing him out the rest of the way. I lifted him into the cat carrier and slammed the lid down on both my own arm and the rod. I had to get my arm out while he was still twisting in the collar. I struggled to loosen it and was worried he was going to hurt himself. The RSPCA inspector shouted hurried instructions as he tried to jump back over the fence to help. I managed to get it loose as the cat twisted again, freeing himself of the collar. I pulled the rod out through the smallest gap under the carrier door I could manage, Louise helping me to press down on the top in case he tried to push it open, allowing me to close and secure it.

As I threw a sheet over the top, he settled down immediately. I rested on the carrier, panting to catch my breath after all the tension.

We thanked the Inspector for his help and rushed the cat back to the veterinary clinic. Getting out of the way, I left the vets to work on him while they did x-rays and gave the pain relief. Soon after, Louise came to tell me that he had *two* broken legs.

Luckily, our fantastic senior orthopaedic vet, Hilary was there that day and happy to take care of him. She was going to have to amputate one leg as it was completely shattered and could not possibly heal. She had to come up with a complicated plan of pins and metal plates to save the other leg, as it was close to also requiring amputation.

In case it did not work, we googled 'cats with two legs' to determine if he would have any quality of life with two amputated legs. YouTube found some great videos of disabled dogs with two legs who ran along like they had never needed four in the first place but we did not manage to find any two legged cats at all. We knew that he would have to be put to sleep if the leg could not be saved.

However, due to the vet's expertise, and possibly some luck that it had not been that little bit worse, the operation was successful. He was unfortunately a three-legged cat then but cats can be quite comfortable on three legs once they get used to it. No owner ever came forward for him so we nicknamed him Linford due to his having been able to run so fast, even with only two working legs.

As he recovered, he showed us his appreciation with mews, brushing himself up against anyone who came to visit him. He could soon move around easily and even jump up into a lap for a cuddle. He was quickly adopted into a loving home with two other disabled cats by a friend of the charity.

Tortie and the Pick-Up Truck

Rescuing Tortie was the first mission that I did alone for C.H.A.T. We were called out to collect an emaciated cat from Barking Road in East London. This is possibly one of the busiest roads in the area. Red double decker buses zoom past every minute and the pavements are frequently so full of people that it is difficult to walk without bumping into them. Smart cats can sometimes live near roads, but you would not want even the smartest of street-smart cats living anywhere near Barking Road.

Knowing that, we thought the cat was likely to be in danger and needed to be collected quickly. I left the clinic immediately with Si the Catman. Si was excellent at his job and was training me at the time, taking me out with him wherever he could. He had endless patience for cats and could out-wait even the most stubborn of cats. The same did not apply to people, however. He would often come back with stories of how he had yelled at someone for getting in his way when he was trying to catch a cat, even if he had been in their house.

The tortoiseshell cat was sitting on a garden wall being stroked by an elderly couple laden with shopping bags. It was clear she (tortoiseshell cats are always female) was completely tame and seemed likely to have had an owner nearby. She did not look very emaciated to me and there was a food bowl on the wall, suggesting she was fed there. She was still dangerously close to the busy road though so we took her back to the clinic to get her checked over. We discovered that she was producing milk, which meant she must have kittens somewhere. This also meant that it was unlikely that she had an owner, as she would surely not be outside on her own if she had kittens at home.

It is always distressing to find out a cat is feeding kittens. There is no way of knowing whether she had been dumped without her kittens or whether they were near where she was picked up, or whether they are even alive but we would always go back to look for them. It was very rare for the charity to find the kittens of a stray cat because mother cats are so good at hiding them, but it was worth the effort. I was determined to somehow find them.

For the rest of that day we searched every garden we could get into within the area. The people who owned the end-terrace garden wall where she had been found did occasionally put food out for her, having assumed she was a stray, but knew nothing about her. I carried a cat basket with me to each house, hoping that this would be the house where we would find her kittens. We spoke to as many people as we could and put up posters on all the lampposts, trees and bus stops in the area. We left our telephone number with every person we met. We asked everyone to keep an eye out and an ear open for crying kittens. This all took place while Tortie was in the clinic being health checked, neutered, microchipped, vaccinated, fleaed and wormed. She went through this because if we did not find her kittens, we would have to return her and, if she had to go back, we wanted her to be in the healthiest possible position.

After several hours of searching we still could not find them. I went back to the clinic with Si to wait, hoping that someone would see our posters, find them and call us before the cat woke up from her anaesthetic. While we waited, we debated whether we should ear-tip her or not. Ear-tipping is done while the cat is under anaesthetic - a small piece is cut from the top of the left ear, leaving it flat at the top rather than pointed. This is done to stray cats so that any rescue centre that sees them in future knows that they are already neutered.

If we were confident that her kittens were still alive, we would ear-tip her and return her to them as soon as it was safe to do so. However, if we felt it was unlikely that her kittens were alive, we would not ear-tip her. Some people feel that it makes a cat less attractive for adoption, so we do not like to do it unless we are certain the cat will not be rehomed. In this case, Tortie was full of fresh milk, and swelling with it through the day, so it had clearly been recently drunk. That meant the kittens were still alive and very well hidden. Therefore, she had the ear-tip.

By the end of the day, no one had called in to say they had found the kittens. We could not leave them much longer without their mother. We waited until around one o'clock in the morning before we took her back. The kittens had been without her for over twelve hours, but they would be ok unless they were newborns. It was necessary to give her plenty of time to wake up fully from the anaesthetic and was also a time when traffic was lightest, putting her least at risk. I took her back along with Celia and two non-rescue evening staff, Pete and Jon.

Pete had been at the charity for years and Celia relied on him to help her out in the evenings. He was super helpful and kind, and I often relied on his help too. Jon was initially a volunteer but was so good with the cats, and the cleaning, and the… everything… that he was taken on as evening staff.

When we got there, we positioned ourselves in different directions to try and follow Tortie to her kittens. The traffic was relatively calm and so we opened the carrier door exactly where we had found her and gave her a big bowl of food. She ate happily and then started rubbing around our legs, asking for attention. We stroked her and soothed her, but she showed no motivation to go anywhere. Maybe her kittens were no longer alive and that was why she was not going to them. Or perhaps she had been dumped there and did not know where she was. Finally, we resolved to not stroke her for a few minutes to see what happened.

After she gave up trying to get more attention, she walked away from us, around the corner into a side street, suddenly sure of where she was going. We followed at a short distance. She jumped up a low front garden wall of a different end-terrace house, then up onto the gate to their back garden, ran along a fence between a small warehouse and the back garden of the same house and disappeared from view. This was one of the same gardens that I had searched earlier that day. It was too dark to see where she had gone beyond the fence and not possible to follow her as we would have to get up on the low wall, and shuffle along the fence or clamber over a tall pile of tyres that had been abandoned, stuffed into a gap, down one side. It was certainly not worth the risk in the dark.

We left a large pile of food by the wall and decided to keep feeding her there in the hope that she would not go close to the road to find food. We also hoped that, if we did not find the kittens soon, when they were old enough she would eventually bring them with her to share the food, giving us a better chance to catch them. It was not ideal but we had done all we could.

As the newest member of the team, I was given the job of putting food down in the same spot and report back any further sign of her.

After two days of the food being eaten without any sighting of her, I had the opportunity to take another look inside the garden of the house immediately to the right of the fence. The surrounding gardens were small and neat without any obvious hiding places. I was sure that the kittens were not in that direction, although if they were not, I could not imagine where they could be. The building to the left of the fence was a car repair garage. I wanted to speak to them to see if they knew anything about the cat, and to check if there was anywhere inside that the cat may have nested with her kittens. But I had driven past it at various times of the day and the garage had never been open. The numbers on the sign above the garage door did not work. I suspected the business had closed down.

The next day, determined to find out where she could have gone, I climbed up on to the low wall surrounding the front garden of the end house, scuffing my knees on the roughness of the bricks. From that height, and on the tips of my toes, I could peer over the fence into the back garden. The smooth, neat lawn made me sure that no cat was likely to run straight across the middle of it. Cats are cautious creatures and like to go around the edge where they can. Spanning the length of the gap between the fence and the garage wall towered a huge stack of tyres. More tyres than you can imagine ever seeing, all squashed into one place. They were held into the gap by a wooden door jammed between the fence and the garage wall. I leaned slightly on the door and it moved, throwing me off balance. I grabbed back onto the fence quickly with both hands to stabilise myself.

I pushed and pulled at the door, wriggling it to see how much it would move. It moved enough to make room for me to squeeze through, if I breathed in. I thought, as I was already there and not busy, I might as well have a look inside some of the tyres to see if there were any hints of where a cat might be nesting. The pile was quite low at that point, only about as high as the wall. Although where it rose further back, it was taller than me in places. That is not saying much, though: I am only five feet tall. I was worried because I had no idea how stable the pile was. It could completely collapse, pushing the door out of its position and slide out into the road in an avalanche, taking me with it and hurting the kittens.

My first step in was particularly cautious. I slowly lowered my weight down on one foot, holding tightly onto the fence and squeezed through the gap. The tyres held. I bounced up and down a little. It seemed safe. Holding even more tightly to the fence, hugging against it, I put all my weight onto the front foot, and brought through my other to join it. It still held. I jumped a little. It seemed fine.

I stepped inside one of the tyres lying flat and found a footing that felt solid. I let go of the fence with one hand and swung my ever-present holdall bag around to my front, rummaging through, I found my torch. It was broad daylight and a beautiful sunny day, with only the occasional cloud, but it would help me to look inside the nooks and crannies. I pulled out a pouch of kitten food as well ready in my pocket. Shrugging my bag back onto my back, I shone the torch inside the edges of each tyre. There was nothing in there except a few old sweet wrappers and a lot of leaves. I peered into the next gaps looking for any suggestions of cats. I steadied myself against the wall as I moved, checking each hole as I went, climbing higher and higher.

At the peak of the pile, I had to crouch low as I was level with the top of the fence. I was quite far along, almost at the end of the wall. I could see over the garden's back fence from that height. I could see into all of the gardens that I had already checked, knowing there was no place in any of them for kittens to hide. I knew I could probably be seen from every house this high up. But who would be looking? If they did see me, and did not recognise me, they might call the police. I thought that I had a good, legitimate excuse for being there, but still hoped that I would not have to explain myself.

I knew I should probably go back. Celia would not be pleased with me taking risks. Although I was quite convinced that the tyres were safe by now as long as I was careful. A slip could probably still do me a lot of damage and leave me stranded where there would be no passer-by. I was sure that I would be fine. I might as well finish what I had started.

I slid down the next few feet, partly on my feet, partly on my bottom as the leaves and muck piled high enough to make a solid surface.

The tyre mountain went down to ground level from there, then back up to higher than before, ending with a pile so high it reached into the hedges. Leaves covered everything so thickly that it almost looked an actual hill. As I was already there I thought that I might as well check right to the end.

On the way up, it became more slippery as the leaves moved underfoot. Despite my caution, I slid, grabbing the top of the fence just in time to stop myself falling, luckily not causing that avalanche that I had so vividly imagined. As I lifted my hand, I felt a splinter come away. I picked at it until it came out.

I had to crawl then, on hands and knees. Finally making it to the end, I peered over a steep drop of debris and leaves. I was astonished to see that the garage had a large yard behind it. It was filled with old, mostly windowless, rusted cars. The wall around the yard was so high, with a thick bush even taller beyond that that I had not been able to see it from any of the surrounding houses. I had not realised that there was a space there.

There was not much chance of my finding any kittens in all that by myself so I started to turn back.

But then, as I had already gone so far, I thought I might as well check just one car, just the closest one.

I clambered down the slope, sliding a little. It conveniently piled up right next to the closest vehicle, a huge, dirty red pick-up truck, the front of it covered with a tarpaulin. I stepped into the back, taking care in case it had corroded through. It held my weight so I climbed in, staying to the edges and holding on. It felt oily under my feet. I remembered Celia telling me about cats giving birth in the foot-well of cars and decided that would be the last place I looked before going back. I inched over in the back of the truck, up to the back window.

Lifting the tarpaulin, there was a hole where the glass window should have been. I stuck my head through it, looking between the seats, wondering if I would have to climb all the way in.

To my absolute delight and surprise, there was a perfectly aligned row of five tiny kittens, snuggled cosily in the foot-well. I noticed movement in the corner of my eye and looked up to find their mum, Tortie, there too, peeping cautiously at me through the unbroken windscreen. Knowing she was friendly, I pulled out the pouch of kitten food and used it to coax her over to me, giving her a stroke to try to let her know I meant her babies no harm. While she ate, I climbed through the missing rear window into the car to check on the kittens. They were only about a week old. Unfortunately a sixth had passed away. I worried that it might be due to our having taken the mother away for the day, but the vets later reassured me that it was the size of a newborn and must have died during the birth. Upsetting, and typical for kittens born stray, but nothing we could do anything about.

Cat Rescuer

I called Celia, 'I found them.'

'Found who?' She asked.

'The kittens.'

'Oh my goodness, that's wonderful! Where are they?' I could hear the excitement in her voice.

'Well, erm... they're in a truck behind that garage that's never open.'

'Oh, is it open then?'

'Erm... no... I kind of climbed those tyres we thought were dangerous... they're more stable than they look and it's not so bad in daylight.' I said quickly, trying to justify getting myself into this situation. 'Except now I am with the kittens and the mother cat is here too and I don't have a basket with me. It's in the van.'

Celia replied, 'Do not leave them. Don't move. The mother will hide the kittens again if you leave them. I'll send someone. Wait there. I'll call you right back.' She hung up.

I fed Tortie another kitten pouch stroking her while she ate it. Fortunately she was hungry enough to keep eating and not get distracted and try to check on her kittens as that would have caused me to restrain her in case she tried to carry one away, which I would prefer not to have to do as it would stress her.

Celia still had not called back as she was finishing the food. While feeding Tortie another pouch, I called her again. She answered, 'Angie's on her way, she'll call you when she gets there.' I hung up to wait, hoping I could keep the mother cat entertained long enough.

Angie worked part-time at the clinic and was thoroughly dedicated to the charity. She had helped out on and off ever since the Sanctuary opened. A committed vegan, she introduced me to many tasty recipes and restaurants over the years, when I previously thought no meal could be good without at least cheese. When she arrived, I felt rather guilty as she was supposed to have finished for the day. She was not happy about having to come rescue me from my adventure. But she knew it was worth it really and I am sure she forgave me quickly. She had to follow where I had climbed, somehow carrying two cat baskets. She managed it and helped me bundle the kittens up safely in one, putting Tortie in the other. We carried one each, back over all the piles of tyres, which turned out to be much more awkward than it had been empty handed.

Back at the van, we loaded both into my vehicle so that Angie could go straight home. The cat and kittens were quite calm all the way. At the clinic, Tortie was obviously happy to be there. Whilst we set her up in a pen for the night, she made the most of the opportunity for attention. She went over to the box filled with blankets where we had placed her five kittens and rubbed her face against their backs, causing them to mew at her and wriggle, blindly looking for her, with their still-closed eyes. They soon wriggled back into a pile, cuddling together, going back to sleep, while she trotted back to the edge of the pen where I was setting up her litter tray. She jumped out of the pen and trotted around me, rubbing against me and pushing her cheek against my arm, almost knocking the tray out of my hand. I gave her lots of strokes in between setting everything up before putting her back into the pen and closing the door. She went straight over to her babies and laid down, so I was confident they would now get a good feed. Going back to the office, I tried to help Celia find a foster home for her, calling around the rehoming officers to see who they thought might be available.

They managed to find someone. It was no one I knew as I had not gotten involved with the fosterers yet. The little family were taken there the next day and all the kittens grew up tame, being rehomed easily once they were eight weeks old. I would like to tell you how they turned out, but this is all I know. There were so many cats and kittens around that they all get merged together in my head. I later discovered that if I needed to be reminded details about who came from where and what they were like, Louise knew every cat that had ever passed through those doors.

Felix and the nine ferals

Many charities do not have the trapping resources that C.H.A.T has. Our specialty was the use of manual traps, where you have to be there physically to trigger the trap at the right moment to catch a specific cat. Most other charities would use the automatic trap option first, which go off automatically when the cat steps on a trigger at the end, with no need for anyone to be there. These charities only contacted us for assistance once this had failed, not having the resources themselves to use the manual trap option, by which time it is often too late for C.H.A.T's manual trapping method to work as effectively.

My first multi-cat trapping job ended up taking much longer than could have been anticipated because of this. The charity was told about nine feral cats that were being fed in a garden. I was apprehensive about trapping so many ferals in one place, so I asked as many colleagues as I could for advice on the best way of dealing with it.

The most useful advice I heard was that if all the cats are the same level of priority (none are pregnant, injured or at risk) then to be patient. The main concern is to make sure that none of the cats see any other cats being caught. If any cat sees another cat being caught, they will become afraid of the trap and it can take weeks or months before they will go in the trap, if they ever will. Even if I was to only catch one cat - the last cat to eat after all the others had left - on the first day, the next day, I could catch the second-to-last. Then, if necessary, catch one a day until all were caught.

It would not always need to be done this way, or take this long. Often we would get two or more cats in the trap at once, or sometimes we could pick up the first cat to arrive as well as the last if the first arrived long enough before anyone else for them to see him caught. Or a cat might eat a little, then wander off, then come back again later. But then again, cats in an established feeding pattern tend to all turn up at the same time, knowing exactly when the food would arrive. This is what happened in my nine feral job.

I dropped off a dummy trap (a trap with no door or trap mechanism) two weeks before I intended to start. The feeders had to feed inside, and only inside, the trap.

The main feeder was the teenage son of the household. His mother was called Jane and she was the one who kept in touch with me, but it was her son who knew the cats, named them and fed them. The whole family were worried about them repeatedly breeding and getting increasingly ill with each new generation. They had recently heard of the Celia Hammond Animal Trust and been told that we would be able to help with their situation. Jane worked caring for the elderly in their own homes locally and so was always nearby to give me access at any time.

The first day of trapping I arrived at midday, an hour before the usual feeding time.

They had a long back garden with a shed on one side near the bottom and a brick summerhouse at the very end on the other side. I set up two manual traps at the same time beside the shed and hid inside the summerhouse to watch.

I counted seven cats. Using both traps at the same time, I managed to successfully catch two cats in each within an hour.

I nearly lost one because I found it difficult to hold both traps closed tight enough at the same time before I could get them locked. I never used two traps again. I felt much more confident with one and was sure I could get all the cats just as easily.

Five of the seven that I had seen were already ear-tipped and so must already be neutered. I decided to take these into the clinic as well, partly to get them out of the way to enable me to identify and trap the remaining cats more easily, and partly because I did not know how or when they had come to be ear-tipped and it was worth taking them in for a vet check. Many charities, including C.H.A.T will microchip stray cats when they neuter them so we might have been able to trace when and where they were neutered.

I gave them all nicknames to help me recognise them, using some of the son's names, and some that I made up myself. A black and white cat, Mr Confident, was always first in the trap. Soon followed by Moustache, also black and white, with a black marking under his nose. Then Granddad would appear and bully everybody else, so he had his turn at the food whenever he wanted it.

Jane was very happy to continue to feed the cats. Her husband and children also loved to watch them play in their garden. Her son was even so kind as to raise their shed onto blocks and build a bed space underneath, so the cats had a dry space to sleep.

Within another two days, I caught another six cats. That made ten out of the expected nine, so far.

All the cats that I had seen were caught and returned. Many of them were completely black, including Granddad, who was eartipped, but had to have a dental as his teeth were unhealthy, showing that it must have been a few years since they were done. None of them had microchips.

Jane often referred to a cat named 'Fluffy' and another called 'Fluffy's sister' (there was no evidence that either were female although Jane's son suspected that both were because they were 'pretty'. Both also black and white.). I had never seen either of these two. I left the dummy trap in the garden for them to keep using until those two would go in too. We had now identified twelve out of the initially suspected nine cats. This was a great example of how easy it is for similar looking cats to trick us.

We needed to find out how some had come to be ear-tipped and so I delivered leaflets to the whole block of approximately one hundred large houses. One lady came out straight after seeing the leaflet come through her door and invited me inside to introduce me to her cat, Felix.

She explained that Felix had appeared in their garden a couple of years ago. They had started feeding her and a few weeks later she turned up with some kittens. These kittens were not very young kittens and were already very nervous of humans, despite their mother's friendly nature. The kittens were too fast to be easily caught so she had only taken Felix to the vet to get her neutered. Borrowing an automatic trap from the vet, she tried to catch the kittens. She had managed to catch some of the kittens, and even a couple of males that had started eating in her garden too, but no matter what she did, she could not catch them all. They became 'trap-shy' and soon the whole group stopped eating in her garden altogether, understandably as each time they did, the trap would catch someone. Felix stuck around regardless, so was taken in permanently.

In my experience, you can never catch a whole colony with an automatic trap as some always become trap-shy, therefore it often fails to reduce a colony sufficiently to prevent further breeding. When using a manual trap, we could be specific. We could catch the pregnant females first, partly because they were very clearly female, and partly to prevent another litter of kittens being born outdoors in an uncomfortable and unhealthy situation. Or we could specify whether we caught kittens first, and then the mother, or the other way around. Or we could catch only an injured male without having to catch the whole colony. It seemed far more time consuming, as we had to spend a lot of time sitting with the trap, but our success rate at neutering whole populations showed that it was worth the effort because we never had to repeat our work.

In theory.

Felix's owner's story explained why some of Jane's cats were ear-tipped and some were not. It also explained why Fluffy and Fluffy's sister were already trap-shy. The family continued to feed the cats in the dummy trap only, but Fluffy and Fluffy's sister would not go into it. They must have been being fed elsewhere as they were never hungry enough to be tempted. We left the trap there for many months, whilst trying to contact a neighbour who we had heard might also feed the cats. The neighbour did not respond to any of the letters we left for her, and the one time I managed to catch her at home, she shut the door in my face. I could not figure out how someone who clearly loved cats so much (I had seen her hallway lined with cat food bowls) could be so unhelpful to someone trying to improve their health and looking out for their welfare.

Months later, Jane called me to let me know that they were still feeding in the dummy trap, but that Fluffy was still eating elsewhere. She told me that her immediate neighbour had opened her back door that morning, horrified to find two dead kittens on the doorstep. This made it very clear that Fluffy or Fluffy's sister, or perhaps both, were actually female. It was uncertain why they had moved their kittens to this doorstep as they had not been there the day before. They would have been about three weeks old and so had not been born there as the neighbour went into her garden everyday with her dog. There was no sign that they had been killed by her dog or another animal apparently. We did not see them as the neighbour buried them in her garden.

We feared that they had died of flu. But we did not know how we could we catch the cats before they became pregnant again, only to have another litter exposed to the same fate.

I took away the dummy trap to see if this would help encourage them back to Jane's garden for now at least. There was no more we could do without the other feeder's help. I posted her a note, written by Celia, explaining about the kittens we had found and why it was more important than ever that we catch them to prevent further deaths, but she still did not respond.

A few months later, Jane called me to say that Fluffy's sister had been in their garden to eat, along with two fluffy kittens! I took the dummy trap back, and the next day, Jane reported that Fluffy's sister had brought both her kittens to eat in the trap. She must finally have gotten over being trap-shy. Either that, or with two babies to feed, maybe she was just too hungry to resist. I arranged to go the day after at about midday, before feeding time, to set up the real trap.

I arrived early and was fully set up before any cats turned up. I hoped that they would not notice that the trap was slightly different from the dummy trap. I sprayed the trap with Feliway (a brand of calming cat-pheromone) and catnip to make it smell like a safe space, and disguise any other differences in smell. Jane had moved the place where she fed the cats closer to the house since I had last been there so I decided to trap from inside the house through the dining room windowed doors. I would be less conspicuous than trying to hide outside.

I waited and waited but there was no sign of Fluffy, or her sister, or any kittens. All the usual crowd turned up though, all looking very healthy. They appeared either over the top of the fence to my left, or from the bottom of the garden near the shed, or through a small hole in the bottom of the fence, very near to the house.

Mr Confident, as usual, was the first in the trap. He was closely followed by two pure black cats that we had neutered already. It was likely the black cats that had caused the initial number confusion. Moustache stalked along the fence up the garden, jumping down next to the trap, pushing out one of the black cats to get his turn.

Then, eventually, not long before it was due to get dark (it was getting dark early at this time of year in late 2010), a little ball of black and white fluff peeked a tiny black nose through the fence. Jane was watching with me out the window and hurried off excitedly to tell the family that it was there again. I was so tense with anticipation that I had to remind myself to breathe.

Then along came Granddad, pushing the kitten aside and coming through the hole himself. What awful timing he had!

Granddad went into the trap to eat. Luckily the kitten had not run off, he put his little head back through the hole and watched Granddad eat. I decided that this might be helpful as the kitten would see that he had no reason to be scared of the trap. After Granddad had finished eating, he went back to the hole. Rather than go through it, he sat washing himself right next to it, blocking it. Every time the kitten tried to get through, Granddad whacked it on the head with his paw.

Eventually Granddad decided he was clean and left. The little kitten hopped through the hole, but rather than going to the food, he found a bit of string to play with, with which he whiled away some time.

It was getting dark and the long back gardens and large houses blocked out much of the light pollution from the streetlights normally prevalent in London. I sneaked out to set up some torches so I would still be able to see, turning them on pointing downwards and then moving the light up slowly so that I would not scare the kitten away. Despite this, it would be increasingly difficult to see the later they came as there were not any other sources of light around.

Fluffy and her sister had not eaten yet. Surely one of them would turn up soon?

The second kitten arrived alone. He was a grey and white ball of fluff with big, dark, watchful eyes. He was beautiful. He hopped through the hole joining the other kitten still playing with the string.

I was watching them play when suddenly another cat jumped through the hole. A pretty longhaired black and white cat that I had never seen before.

Jane was back at the window with me and explained that this was definitely Fluffy and not her sister. Apparently they were almost identical, except Fluffy's sister was less fluffy. We had assumed Fluffy's sister was the mother, as she had led them to the food the day before, although we had no way of knowing for sure. I thought perhaps Fluffy could be their mother herself as she was with them today, but her long fur and the advancing darkness made it difficult to see whether she was swollen with milk to know if she was feeding kittens or not.

She walked straight into the trap, and I resolved to catch her if the kittens went into the trap too. I could not catch just her as the kittens would see. Even if she did turn out to be their mother, it was better to have caught her and the kittens and got them back the clinic safely, and catch the others later. This was exactly what happened, she went into the trap and both kittens followed her in. By this time it was very dark and I had to strain to check no other cats were watching. It was a risk, but I had an adult cat and two kittens in the trap, with no others in sight. How could I let them go now? I closed the trap.

As the trap banged shut, I was sure I saw a kitten-sized grey shape run past the hole in the fence. But it was too late, I had to secure and cover the trap quickly and would have to wait to find out if there really was a third kitten. I ran out as quickly as I could, grabbing the torch and shining it into the neighbour's garden to figure out if I really had seen a kitten. I could see an outline of an adult cat sitting watching me at the other side of the garden in the dark, but could not figure out who it was, it looked too big and not fluffy enough to be the one I thought I had just seen.

I was so sure I had seen some grey fluff in that moment. I could not shake the worry that perhaps there were more kittens than the two that Jane and her son had seen the day before. I resolved to stay longer and see if anyone else turned up. At the very least Fluffy's sister might wander over. I transferred Fluffy and the two kittens into more comfortable cages and hid them out of the way, then set the trap back up and settled back in to wait.

I had been there so long that I had missed lunch and dinner, and had only brought cereal bars with me. Jane very kindly offered me some lovely homemade pumpkin soup and I sat and ate this gratefully stood by the window, while her family ate at the table. It was nice to be looked after.

I had only just finished my soup, when a black and white fluffy kitten jumped through the hole. This had me very confused as it was not grey at all. Jane was absolutely certain that there had only been two kittens, but now I was wondering if there could be four. This kitten looked so similar to the black and white one we had already caught that we reasoned perhaps she had seen two at different times and would not have realised.

Another adult cat then came through the hole that I did not recognise.

Jumping up, June exclaimed, 'That's Fluffy's sister!'

She walked straight into the trap, as though she had been doing this all along, and not been taunting me for months. The black and white kitten followed her straight in. There were no other cats or kittens watching that I could see, and I waited a minute while they ate, just in case. But I knew they would be getting full and I could not leave it long, so I caught them. I transferred them over to join their little family and now I had a decision to make.

I was so sure that I had seen grey fur in that moment, not black. There must still be another kitten. It was after nine in the evening and I should have been finishing work by then. But I could not bring myself to even entertain the risk of leaving a kitten overnight all by itself as I must certainly now have its mother, whether she was Fluffy or her 'sister'.

Jane was convinced that there were no more, but agreed to let me stay a while longer. I set the trap back up, and dug out a tin of extra smelly food from my bag, soon to become my favourite trapping food – sardines!

After half an hour, I was beginning to think I should go. Although Jane's family did not say anything, they must have been wanting me out of their house by then so that they could get on with whatever they usually did in the evening.

Whilst I was thinking this, a grey and white longhaired kitten jumped through the hole, immediately circled the trap looking for the entrance, then walked in, without a fear in the world.

Catching him in the trap straight away, I reunited him with the other kittens and took the whole family back to the clinic. I left more food down and gave Jane's family strict orders to watch as much as possible, just in case there were even more kittens.

Jane gave me a bottle of wine as a thank you for all the effort I had made to help her much-loved strays, which was very sweet of her.

A few days later, she confirmed there were no more. They had been watching frequently every day and not seen any. I had now caught sixteen cats since being called about nine. The whole colony was finally done and could live out their days getting fat, lazing in the sun.

Before returning Fluffy and her sister back to Jane, we had quite a difficult task ahead of us. They had been with us for three weeks and the sisters (both were female) had been neutered. Fluffy's sister had been confirmed to be the mother as she was the one with milk. Fluffy had not been pregnant or feeding kittens. The kittens were over eight weeks old and theoretically ready for rehoming. The problem was that the whole family were completely feral.

Fluffy was so scared that she reacted violently to people being anywhere near her. Fluffy's sister was not violent, but was so terrified that she would cower into a corner at anyone's approach. We had hoped that the two could be rehomed, each with one of the kittens or perhaps with each other, as they were so close. But we could not get around them to tame the kittens as they would attack, biting and scratching.

Thankfully, Jane agreed to take back the two sisters. After all, she said, that was their home and at least they would still have each other. Jane could remember the first time they had turned up as kittens themselves. We needed to give them a second vaccination before they were returned so that they would have maximum protection against the flu.

The biggest threat in an overpopulated colony is cat flu. It only takes one cat to catch a flu and the whole colony might have it permanently. If kittens are still being born into the colony, they will re-infect the adults too. A vicious cycle.

Cat Rescuer

Many will recover from the flu, but even those can be permanently damaged by bronchitis or other breathing difficulties, or infected or missing eyes. This is not rare. Cat flu is a daily encounter for a cat rescue charity. It is found in every overpopulated group of cats. It is so common that the charity would have at least one whole room of cats ill from flu at any one time. It's usually the largest room, if only one. Sometimes it felt as if every cat we picked up had flu. A neutered colony tends to throw off the flu quite quickly (even if not vaccinated), if they catch it at all, as all are strong, fed, healthy adults with no new kittens being born to catch it and pass it on.

Celia was an expert with ferals and was known for being able to cuddle cats that no one else could get anywhere near. So it was left to her to get that second vaccine into poor feral Fluffy. I agreed to help. The sisters would not let us split them up to make it easier for us, they would move together around the pen as though they were one cat. Celia decided to try to vaccinate them nevertheless, she said that they could lean on each other for comfort while she did it. It was a mistake. Fluffy bit her. Badly.

Celia was bitten and scratched frequently. But I could tell this was worse simply because she was not ignoring it completely as she usually would. She kept saying 'oooo' and 'ouch' every few seconds and holding onto it, squeezing the tissue against it. There was a worrying amount of blood. The vaccine was done though, so Celia was satisfied. Wrapping a thick bandage of tissue around her hand, she went back to work on her emails.

The next day Celia's hand was swollen to twice the size and she had to take antibiotics. I am sure Celia will still remember that cat and say the bite was my fault, because it was my trapping job… if only I were brave enough to vaccinate a feral myself.

Once the cats had been returned to Jane, the kittens were able to be tamed (mostly) and were rehomed in two pairs only a couple of weeks later to new owners that were well aware of their nervousness and happy to tame them the rest of the way.

The charity was insistent on rehoming all cats in pairs. That is, all cats that like other cats, of course. I would often be asked, 'Surely it is better to rehome one cat than none at all?'

This is how I had felt too when I first started working there. Over those educational years, I came to realise that the charity was right to rehome the way it does. Pairs of cats are so much happier together than alone. They also seemed to settle in quicker and have a more homely routine, rather than being out all the time, which many people preferred. Perhaps cats that live alone wander off to find and socialise with other cats. The number of owned cats I have accidentally caught when I have found them 'hanging out' with a colony of ferals certainly seems to lend credence to this theory. Also, pairs of kittens are easier to look after than a single kitten because they entertain each other. Much better than them using the curtains as toys.

The story of the nine ferals was not over yet. Another six months later, Jane called me saying worriedly, 'Nichola, there are more kittens!'

I asked, 'How can there be? We neutered everyone.'

Jane had not seen any adult cats that were not ear-tipped since we last spoke. Only four new, pure black kittens.

They were not nearly as nervous as most of the cats and one would apparently even eat from a spoon held out by her son. Jane asked around and confirmed that they did not belong to anyone. By this time she had gotten to know many of the cat sympathisers in the area and had become known for 'her ferals'. The neighbours all appreciated her for taking action to stop the number of them increasing further.

I caught all four easily in one afternoon. There really were four this time. They were too nervous to be owned but had clearly been more socialised than most of the other cats in the colony. I thought someone must know them.

They were already about six months old and so must have been born shortly after we returned Fluffy and her sister. Jane and her family had already fallen in love while watching them play all day and were happy to have them back. I asked them to keep an extra careful eye out for the cat that we must have missed, and to check that every cat was ear-tipped to try to work out who could be their mother.

A few weeks later, I was going back through our Problem Book in the office, double-checking that we had dealt with all the emergencies. I came across a call from a lady who lived around the corner from Jane in Stoke Newington. She had left a message saying she had a cat with kittens in her garden shed. At that point in the year, at the start of summer, it felt as if there were kittens being born in every garden in London. We simply were not able to get to all of them, which is why these kittens had not been on the emergency list, and why no one had brought the call to my attention.

I called the lady, the four kittens were all black. They had disappeared a few weeks ago, then returned a week later with their ears tipped. Sound familiar?

I asked if she knew the mother cat. She had been feeding her every day for about a year. The puzzle was solved. She was more than happy to let me trap in her garden, and was even willing to keep the mother after she had been neutered.

On day one of attempting to trap 'Miss Elusive', I got a quick glimpse of her – she had all the same markings as

Moustache, including the dark mark under her nose. Perhaps I had confused her for him in the past - and then she disappeared and did not return again all evening.

On day two, she did not show up at all.

On day three, I left a dummy trap and asked the lady to feed inside this for a while, as clearly this cat was smart.

On day four, the feeder let me know that Miss Elusive had turned up but would not eat the food if it was anywhere near the trap. I asked her to feed her as close to the trap as she would accept it, and each day, move it a bit closer to the trap.

This plan worked wonderfully and only two weeks later, Miss Elusive was eating in the back of the trap.

I turned up with the manual trap shortly before her usual feeding time.

Miss Elusive did not show up.

She was much too clever to be fooled by my usual technique of trapping. I was no longer a novice, I was now highly experienced and had personally caught hundreds of cats using this method so her shrewdness fascinated me. This cat was one of a kind and was not falling for it. I would have to up my game. I do love a challenge.

By now, Miss Elusive was learning to trust the feeder quite a lot and would willingly eat right beside her. It was time to take advantage of this. Although this might temporarily break this poor cat's trust of her feeder, she would soon forgive her.

Using the same dummy trap that was already being used, I made a few adjustments and left a door for it, turning it into an adapted version of a manual trap. I gave her strict instructions; 'Do not close the trap unless the cat is all the way at the far end,'

'Do not close the trap until her tail is fully inside,'

'Do not close the trap if she looks nervous and ready to bolt because it will not close in time.'

To be honest, I did not like leaving someone else to do this, cats are faster than many give them credit for. I was good at trapping. I knew the rules intuitively by now and I could not afford for this one to go wrong. But Miss Elusive was not going to let me catch her any other way. The feeder seemed very sensible and did listen carefully. I asked her to call me if she had any further questions and called her the next day to go over all the rules again, although she had understood perfectly and was clearly going to be fine.

Only two days later, I got the phone call, 'I've got her!'

I hurried straight there, hoping that nothing would go wrong before I could get there. Miss Elusive was in the trap when I arrived, happily curled up at one end. She looked comfortable and was pretending that she had been easy to catch. What was it about this colony that they liked to mock me?

I used cable ties around the locks to seal the trap safely shut to be certain she would not be able to escape on the way back to the clinic. From my first visit to a colony with an estimated population of nine, it had taken me almost two years to catch the total of twenty-one cats.

Miss Elusive was health-checked, neutered, vaccinated, microchipped, ear-tipped, fleaed, wormed and then returned to her feeder where she lived very happily ever after.

If only the manual trap had been used from the start, none of the cats would ever have gotten trap-shy in the first place. It is unfortunate that the first charity that was contacted did not either use this method or contact C.H.A.T to deal with the situation from the start. Lives would have been saved.

Nichola Kirk
Daisy in the Shoebox

One summer afternoon, after a busy morning at the veterinary clinic, a gentleman walked in carrying a shoebox. The man explained that his dog had been sniffing obsessively at the box on the Greenway, a walking and cycling route that follows the pipelines around East London. As he approached, he had heard a rustling movement as though something was inside the box. Opening it up, he had found that it contained a puppy.

'Oh', I thought, 'it must be a very small puppy to fit inside such a small shoebox.'

Taking the box into a consulting room, we opened it to find a tiny Staffordshire Bull Terrier puppy. It was immediately obvious how she had ended up abandoned. One eye was brown; the other a cloudy white. At ten days old, she would have just opened her eyes for the first time for her owner to discover that she was blind in one of them. Added to that, she had a very unattractive hole in her face between her nose and her mouth — a hare-lip. Her veterinary bills would also potentially be high if either the eye or the lip were to cause problems. She would certainly not have been easy to sell. A breeder had clearly abandoned her to die to save themselves the trouble and expense.

I had already come across various reasons to be against breeding. There are so many homeless animals already. Why bring more animals into the world when you could be helping to find homes for the ones that are already alive and unwanted? I added this poor puppy's experience to my mental list of reasons to be against the breeding of pets.

I immediately fell in love with the puppy. She was beautiful to me.

She was smaller than my hand, and I have very small hands. She was going to need bottle-feeding. I had hand-fed kittens in the past and knew how difficult it could be. Nevertheless, I offered to have the puppy live with me with the help of Wendy, another dog-lover. Wendy was one of the receptionists and she had started working at the charity around the same time as me. She was about my height of five-foot with a short, dark bob of hair. Wendy had three dogs of her own. I credit much of my survival at the charity to Wendy as she went through very similar experiences to me. We suffered together the extraordinary workload, the stress of having to tell people 'no' over the phone, even when we knew they were desperate for our help. We moaned about it, but it was all worth it for the good we could do and we endured it together.

We named our foster puppy Daisy. She was a dark brindle colour all over other than the white flower shape on the back of her neck.

I researched hand-rearing puppies with hare-lips and found an excellent article telling me to use a syringe to feed her to begin with. I needed to ensure the milk went to the back of her mouth, past the hole, to ensure she would not accidentally aspirate any milk into her lungs. This could cause pneumonia. The article also stated that no matter what I did, this would almost certainly happen anyway.

Daisy was too young to regulate her own body temperature and so I had to make sure she was kept warm constantly. This meant re-heating a hot water bottle every few hours and checking it often to make sure it was warm enough.

I kept up hourly feeds all that day to try to build her strength back to where it should have been if she had not been abandoned.

Celia was worried that I would not be able to continue rescue work at the same rate whilst caring for Daisy. I was sure that I could do both. Daisy came with me to a cat pick-up, riding in the van in a carrier strapped into the front seat. She came with me to a trapping job, where I fed her whilst waiting for a cat to turn up. She came with me to lunch, where I had bites of my sandwich between feeding her milk. She seemed to be doing well.

Until about ten o'clock that first evening.

She started breathing heavily, gasping for breath. Then she went limp and stopped breathing altogether. I jumped up and ran through the clinic, rushing to find the nurse on-call, who was luckily still in the building. The nurse called the vet asking her to hurry back. She kept the phone pressed to her ear against her shoulder while she swung my Daisy upside-down, holding her tiny body with both hands, trying to clear her lungs and encourage her to breathe. After every few swings she would wipe Daisy's nose and rub her chest vigorously with two fingers. It was horribly distressing to watch her tiny body being handled in this way. In between, the vet arrived and gave her various injections to help clear any fluid from her lungs and keep her heart beating. I winced as each needle went in, despite knowing she was unconscious and could not feel them.

I had been warned that her survival chances were slim but I had been so hopeful that she would live. They kept at it for longer than perhaps they would normally have considering her low survival chances, probably because I was there, trying to keep out the way, clinging onto a surgery room doorframe, clenching my teeth and bouncing on my toes, feeling desperate but useless. I think that they kept at it as they could not bear to tell me that it was hopeless.

But, incredibly, amazingly, wondrously, Daisy started breathing by herself again.

The vet tried to manage my expectations, warning me that she was lucky to be alive and there was a good chance that Daisy would crash again and she was unlikely to survive it next time. I was devastated, but still held onto that little bit of hope that she had pulled through this time, resolute to do everything in my power to keep her going.

I took her home shortly afterwards and continued her hourly feeds through the night. The alarm clock would go off every hour, at which point I would boil the kettle to mix the milk. Then I had to cool it in cold water to the correct temperature. I had to feed her drop by drop with a syringe until she had had at least one millilitre. She did not take it easily, I had to encourage her mouth open for each drop. Sometimes she would not swallow and the milk would stay in her mouth. This put her at huge risk of inhaling it as it could easily get into her lungs through the hole caused by the hare-lip in the roof of her mouth. I had to rub her throat to encourage her to swallow. The whole night passed by painstakingly slowly and wearyingly. Drip… swallow… drip… swallow… drip… swallow.

By the time she had finished a feed, I would lay down for what felt like only minutes before the alarm would sound and I would have to get up again to get the next milk ready. I stayed on the sofa and napped whenever I could, hanging one hand over the edge of the sofa, wrapped around Daisy so that I could feel her breathe and keep her warm. At nine the next morning, she was alive. We had made it through the night.

I was exhausted. Iris, on reception, was already hand-rearing some kittens, so fed Daisy for me to give me a short rest. She was the best and most experienced hand-rearer we had and so I knew Daisy was in very good hands. She had short, dark hair and the friendliest manner. She would make friends with regular clients, human and animal alike and was well-liked.

Wendy took Daisy home that night. She told me the next morning that she had crashed again. The vets had managed to bring her round but she had been unconscious for even longer than the first time. Over those first few days we barely managed to keep her alive. But we did.

Another week passed and Daisy was on her feet, although wobbly and unstable. She had started to accept the syringe happily, realising that it provided food, which made feeding her much easier. She was also strong and alert enough to swallow too. We reduced the feeds to every other hour.

She was getting stronger by the day and wanted to learn to walk, but she was unable to do so without slipping. I had laminate floors in the flat and Daisy could not get a grip on it. I collected all my rugs and towels and laid them beside the sofa to help her move around a little. I put up a barrier of cardboard at one end so she could not go too far. When she had walked to the edge of the rugs and ended up on the laminate floor, she would sit down and cry pitifully. It was the most heart-breaking little noise, like a mouse trying to howl. I put her back in the middle. She would run a few steps on the rugs, but quickly end up on the laminate again and sit down, crying. She did not understand that she needed to stay on the rugs and was so excitable that she never stayed on them for very long at all, I could not help but laugh as I moved her back again and again. She refused to try to walk on the laminate and demanded to be picked up every time, even once she was much more stable and probably could have managed it.

As she grew, we taught her to play. My partner loved her too and we would spend hours playing tug or rolling a ball. We would sometimes forget that she could not see out of one eye and wonder for a moment why she had not chased the toy, until we realised that she had not seen it move. We had to make sure to roll the toy on the side she could see or she would just sit down waiting for the toy to appear. She also loved to bite the nose of a particular teddy that we used for her to sleep, or she would wrestle it, flipping it around.

No matter how hard I tried, she never learnt to wee on the puppy pad. They did not work for us at all. Whenever we thought she had figured it out we would cheer and she would toddle over for a cuddle, excitedly wagging her tiny tail. Then the next time, she would go right next to the pad and still ran over to us wagging her tiny tail excitedly asking for praise. Or, more frequently, tear up the pad with her teeth and pee on the floor where it had been. She was very mischievous. She was so adored by us all that we could not help but let her get away with anything and she quickly learnt how to manipulate us. She spent most days in the office of the clinic, and all the staff and volunteers would sneak her treats all day, making it impossible to teach her anything.

At eight weeks old, she was still so small that she could walk underneath Wendy's Jack Russell. I was reluctant to give her up, and ended up researching everything from living with dogs in flats, to getting my own place so that she could stay with me.

In the end, shortly before she had her second vaccination at twelve weeks old, a supposedly good home came up. Angie, who had helped me carry the kittens over the tyres on my first rescue, was the most experienced at dog home-checks and came up from the Sanctuary in Hastings especially at Celia's request. She took me with as Celia must have known that I would not give Daisy up unless the home was flawless.

They were a lovely couple, with two large, happy dogs, living by a huge park. They were willing to dedicate themselves to Daisy and do whatever was necessary to ensure her happiness. I accepted that it would be years before I could be a dog owner realistically. I was far too involved in my job to be available often enough to provide a good home for a dog. The family seemed so perfect for her that I had to accept that Daisy would be better off with them. She moved in with the couple just after her second vaccination. I missed her so much, I felt like I'd lost a part of myself. I still miss her but I know that it was the right decision for Daisy's sake.

The charity had offered to get her hare-lip repaired when she was old enough, and operate on her eye if she ever developed the glaucoma. She did initially have some trouble with some solid foods, but the family tried different foods until they found the types that she could eat easily, and her eye never got any worse. Ultimately, they decided it was not worth putting her through either operation as she was getting along beautifully and they had become nothing more than superficial imperfections. Her new owners gave us regular updates for a while afterwards and reported back that their other Staffy had taken over as a mother figure for our little Daisy, and their male Great Dane was bossed around by her. They toilet trained her easily compared to the debacle we had gone through with her, although I maintain that they had an advantage in that they had a garden and good role models and did not have to resort to apparently chewable puppy pads. She had the happiest life that we could ever have wished for but I will always remember her.

Cat Rescuer

Casper and the string

A man called the charity to let us know that he had been walking down a street in East Ham and had seen a white cat with something caught around its leg and a horrendous smell coming from it. He had not been able to get anywhere near it. At the time my favourite trapping food was warm kippers in butter. I am sure butter is bad for cats considering that they are lactose intolerant but it seemed to help keep the kippers warm for longer and help carry the scent further so I used it occasionally in emergencies. I warmed some up quickly in the microwave and hurried to meet the man. But by the time I arrived on the street, there was no sign of the man or the cat.

The office updated me that he had to go, so they gave me his number. I called the man but he was not able to come back to show me where he had last seen the cat as he was on his way to work, so he tried to describe it. I found where I thought he must be talking about and knocked on a couple of doors to try to narrow down where the cat may have gone and find out if it might be owned. No one knew of it or had seen it until I found an end-terrace house, with a gap between it and the next set of terraced houses. Some builders were working on it, who thought they might have seen the cat go past them into the back gardens. They allowed me through. The large garden had a hedge on the left, a four-foot-high wall at the back and down the right hand side. Tip-toeing against the garden wall, I held my phone high, taking photos of the back-to-back gardens that stretched as far as the eye could see (some of the streets in East London are very long) and texted them to Celia. When she called me, I explained despairingly, 'This is hopeless. If the cat was here at all, it could be anywhere now.'

We had a suspicion that the smell coming from the cat could be caused by an infection, meaning that whatever was caught around its leg had been there a while and was causing serious harm to the cat. If the cat was stray, which seemed likely as an owner had not removed the foreign object, without treatment the infection would be likely to spread and could be fatal. That was if the flies did not get there first, laying their eggs in the infected flesh, which would hatch into maggots then eat the poor animals' flesh.

We agreed that I might as well give it a go as I was there already with the warm kippers and despite the low chances of my coming across the cat, the benefits of catching such a potentially at-risk cat far outweighed any costs.

I set up my trap at the bottom of the garden and rested on the back doorstep to wait.

I am not a fan of fish generally, but the kippers smelled tasty even to me. They were still warm enough that the smell would travel. I hoped the scent might even catch the cat up and encourage him back.

I waited for quite a while, and my stomach had just started to rumble when I heard rustling a few gardens along. Cats do not normally make noise. They are more likely to pop up unexpectedly and silently than they are to make a sound so I was curious as to what could be there.

Standing up slowly and quietly, I peeked over the hedge to see what was there. I could not see anything, so I settled back down.

I saw it then, through the hedge to the left. It was a white, dirty-looking cat with the typical puffy cheeks of an unneutered male. He tried to jump high enough to get onto the wall at the back that ran along both gardens. It should have been an easy jump, but he seemed to be having trouble getting up there. I could not yet see what was causing the problem, what exactly he was entangled in or how badly.

After a few single-minded attempts, he made it up and sat on the top of the wall. There was still no obvious sign of any injury or object that might be causing his difficulty from that angle. I wondered if this was the correct cat.

I stayed as still as I could, trying not to meet his eyes as he watched me. Maintaining immobility is an acquired skill, it turns out. When I first started trying to be more patient than a cat, I often lost as I am naturally quite restless and fidgety. But it became increasingly possible, with practice. I learnt that I would only have to wait longer for them if I moved at all. There was no place for me to hide, so I had to hope that my presence alone would not be enough to scare him off. Luckily for me, he was not a feral cat.

I named him before even catching him. He was the first white cat I had to catch, so I thought Casper would suit him nicely, if he was not owned of course.

He cautiously watched me for a few minutes, but soon decided he would rather have the food than worry about why I was there. He jumped down from the wall and I was able to see the problem - a trail of about three feet of tangled string, dragging behind him, catching on branches and grass and tied worryingly tight around his back leg. His leg looked even dirtier than the rest of him, covered in wet pus.

I could not be sure if someone had done this to him intentionally, or if he had just been unlucky and gotten himself tangled. Either way, I knew he needed me so I would not be going anywhere until I had caught him.

I had put a white sheet over the back of the trap, as I often did, to help me see whether a cat is inside the trap or behind it, as it is not always clear, especially in poor light or from a long distance. Casper tugged at this sheet, lifting it, trying to get to the food. It ended up falling on him, scaring him and he ran back to the edge of the garden, looking like he might jump back over the wall, but just for a second. Then he came again. He circled the trap, dragging his string along with him. I worried he might end up getting tied to the trap if the string caught it as he went around it.

He missed the entrance to the trap completely but then somehow managed to push his way under the sheet again. He cunningly put his front paws through the gaps in the trap, pulling bits of food out. Most cats get bored of this very quickly and will look again for a better way in. But Casper seemed quite happy to keep accessing the food in this way. I guess it meant he would not have to walk anywhere. Walking must have been painful for him, with having to drag his leg, and the string and the trail of debris along too. At least this way he got to sit and to eat. I needed to act before he ate too much or he would have no reason to go in the trap at all. I approached slowly, crouching, giving him time to back off. He hurried to the corner of the garden, ready to jump up the wall if he decided I was threatening. He seemed to be delaying jumping up though. I think it was too awkward and painful for him, which in this case worked in my favour.

I turned the trap around and rearranged the sheet until it was tucked tightly under the trap. Then I put extra kippers on the door of the trap and laid a trail of food, which should lead him in. As I move back, he started forward again straight away.

Casper did not walk in the straight line that I had expected back to the trap, he circled it instead, ending up at the wrong end again and tried to get back under the sheet. I had tucked it under tightly enough and he soon had to start looking for another way in.

He finally found the door and licked up some of the kippers. By now I was sitting with my fingers crossed, my breath held. He noticed the next bit of kipper along. He ate it very slowly, then licked the wooden door for any crumbs. Noticing the next piece of the trail, he took a step forward to reach the next bite. I started to breathe again, he was going in the right direction. I was hoping, praying, that he would see the next piece of food. I need not have worried. He had figured it out by then. He ate the next piece, and the next, and then was far enough along that he could see the big pot of food at the end. He hurried the rest of the way in.

I closed the trap, excitedly exhaling 'Got him!' to myself.

The men who were working in the house had been watching through the window. They came out to congratulate me as I locked the trap thoroughly and covered it. They carried the trap with Casper inside into my van for me.

His story was clearly popular news at the clinic, as I walked past the reception window, everyone was looking at me expectantly. I pushed into the office door with the trap in my arms. There was a collective sigh of relief. They had all been worrying.

I handed him over to the vets still in the trap, explaining what I had seen of the string, while I stood back and watched the nurse lift the sheet. She immediately dropped it again taking a step back and holding her nose, 'Oh, he smells terrible,' she said. 'He must have a really bad infection'. My sense of smell is not that good. That worked in my favour many a time walking into homes with too many cats, trying to politely tolerate that intense smell of ammonia caused by large numbers of litter trays.

The nurses prepared an operating room and went to test Casper's friendliness while I wrote up his information sheet.

The C.H.A.T nurses were highly experienced with feral and nervous cats and knew how to approach them to minimise the risk of attack. As soon as they put a hand on Casper, he started to purr. He pressed himself against the nurse's hand and was clearly relieved to be back in the company of nice humans. He must have known we were going to help him. Or maybe he was hoping for more kippers.

He had to be put under anaesthetic because the string was so tight that it had cut right through to the bone and was so badly infected that the skin had started to die and fall off, leaving flesh and bone exposed, which all had to be stitched and repaired.

He had clearly been in this state for a while so he must not have a home, or they would surely have taken the string off by now. As he recovered, all the nurses came to love him. All the reception staff came to love him. All the volunteers came to love him. And of course, I came to love him. His injury was so severe that he remained in intensive care for months. I visited him every day. It seemed that he could purr ceaselessly.

One Monday, I came in to work to find he had been rehomed over the weekend. Although I did not get to meet his new owners, I knew he would have gone to an excellent home. I appreciated the efforts of the rehoming officers and knew they had very high standards.

Bob in Central London

Responding to a call from central London where a cat had collapsed in a conservatory, I got there as fast as I could, which unfortunately was not particularly fast, considering central London traffic. It took me about an hour even though it was only seven miles away. The frustration I experienced of knowing that the cat needed me urgently made me wish for ambulance style lights, sirens and privileges to move past the traffic. I could see no reason why animal ambulances should not have these. When I finally arrived, I found the poor thing curled up under a chair. I lifted the cat carefully into a carrier, its whole body hanging limply, asking questions in the process. Had he seen the cat before? Had he fed it? What had happened for it to get here? I was reluctant to waste time finding out the detail, we could do that on the phone later. I needed to get him to a vet immediately. I did manage to find out that the man who had called, who owned the conservatory, had never fed the cat before but had seen it once before the day before when it had apparently looked fine. He had assumed it was owned and shooed it away. It had turned up today and promptly collapsed under the chair. As I rearranged the blanket in the carrier to support him and keep him comfortable, I noticed a collar with the name 'Bob'.

The drive back to the veterinary clinic was exasperating as I tried to find the quickest routes around the traffic. I had put the carrier on the front seat, seat-belted in, so that I could keep an eye on Bob. He was deteriorating quickly and felt cold despite the warm weather, so I put the heaters on full blast. I had to get through bad central London traffic, which was painstakingly slow. When we were only half-way back, I was sure he had died. But there was nothing I could do.

When I arrived back at the vets, after what felt like the longest drive of my life, but can only have been half an hour,

I explained to the head vet, 'I am quite certain that he has already passed away, but would you mind having a look anyway?'

To my relief, he was still alive, but only just. The vets and nurses started to rush around him, grabbing medicines and drips to help him. They rubbed honey on his gums to give him a quick sugar boost to help keep him going, as the vet suspected he was dying of starvation.

Once they had done everything they could and his heartbeat was a little stronger, they wrapped him up warmly, with tubes coming out of him and left him with a nurse to watch him in a calm, quiet room.

We took Bob's collar off and found a telephone number on there. Bob turned out to be an indoor cat, who had jumped out a window, probably looking for female cats, and not been seen since. They turned out to live only about two streets away from where he had been found, but far enough that he might not have been able to find his way back if he had never been out before. We told them of his condition and his owner burst into tears and insisted on coming to see him straight away. They cuddled him, crying anxiously, devastated by what had happened.

They then came every single day to see him in the intensive care ward until he was well enough to go home, and in the meantime prepared their house by installing cat nets over their windows so he could be safely kept indoors and had him neutered to reduce his temptation to go out in the first place.

The Bracelet

I went to pick up a cat with a collar stuck under its leg late one evening. The caller advised me that she had put food out for the local strays each day as usual, when she had noticed an owned cat that was pregnant. She had not done anything about her because she had been wearing a collar and so must be owned, but the collar had been caught around her leg for at least a week. She had assumed that the owner, or whoever had put the collar on the cat in the first place, would remove it. However, a week later with it still stuck, and still pregnant, she decided that the cat must have been abandoned or was being neglected and that she had better do something about it.

She had then tried to lure the cat into her own cat's basket to catch her, but the cat had been too nervous for her to be able to get hold of. She assured me that the cat would come near us, but not within reach. I set the trap a small distance away, further along the path to her doorway, and stood with the lady on the doorstep of her flat.

She insisted that I use the fresh chicken that she had bought specially to tempt the cat with, and so I placed a trail of this going into the trap. She then proceeded to make me and her guest a cup of tea, and we stood chatting for a little while, whilst waiting for the cat to appear, about their past exploits catching cats with Celia.

I always timed my visits around the usual feeding time of the cat that I wanted to catch, as I had in this case, so we were not waiting long before the cat appeared out from under a car in the nearby car park for the flats.

I could not see the collar from that distance but could tell she was very round. Sitting next to the car, she sniffed the air. I was not sure if she was sniffing to try to figure me out or sniffing to find out what food we were offering. She watched us while a big ginger cat arrived (already neutered apparently) and ate some of the food in the trap.

The ginger tom came over to us and was rubbing himself around each of our legs, taking it in turns to get as much attention as he could, when the female cat started to come over. It was awful watching her try to walk. She was caught in the collar so tightly that she could not use that leg properly and so was limping, while at the same time, she was so heavily pregnant that she was waddling too. It was a very awkward sort of limp-hobble-walk. I wanted to go to her and help her but thought that she was not likely to let me, and I could help her soon if I could catch her.

I was amazed at how she had been managing to keep herself without being able to move very quickly. Thank goodness we had been called or she would have had to give birth with that collar stuck under her leg. She might not have been able to reach around when giving birth to break the sacs of the kittens and clean them. She waddle-limped her way up to the trap but could not work out how to get in. She went around the back first to look at the food, then looked up at us. Since working with cats so closely, I had come to understand cat body language quite well, and interpreted this to mean, 'I would appreciate some help here, can't you people see that I am disabled?'

I walked over to her slowly, giving her time to back off. She backed away at the same pace maintaining the distance between us. I turned the trap around for her and moved away again. She came forward again at the same rate that I backed off. This time she was able to figure the trap out. But still she took her time over every piece of chicken, almost seeming to savour and appreciate each bite.

Nichola Kirk

I caught her once she was all the way inside the trap, but she was very frightened and I had to cover the trap very quickly to calm her. I was tempted to look at the extent of the collar wound damage there but decided it would be best to resist curiosity and leave the cover over her to help her stay calm until we were back at the clinic.

The kind lady handed out more chicken for me to take back for the cats in the shelter, which was very considerate of her and was much appreciated by the cats.

When I got back, it was late so Celia helped me to carry the trap with the collar wound cat inside into a consulting room to assess her temperament whilst waiting for the vet. We were pleased to find that up close, she had remembered that she was tame and let us handle her easily, almost happily.

The wound though was much worse than we had expected considering the collar had only been caught for just over a week. It seemed an odd sort of black elastic collar and had rubbed its way into the cat's skin, which had promptly scabbed over the top of many stretches of the elastic, most noticeably under her left armpit and the right of her neck, where it was pulling against her skin the tightest.

There was no way we were going to be able to remove it without cutting the skin so when the vet arrived, she had to be put under anaesthetic. It was my last job of the evening, so I stayed in the clinic to assist the on-call vet and nurse as I felt guilty for bringing in an emergency so late in the evening (not that I had done this intentionally of course). The vet had to cut through lots of her skin to get the collar out from under it. He then had to cut even more skin away where it had gotten infected already.

As he cut the other side out, he pulled out and laid on the table not a collar, but a bracelet. It was a string of crystal covered beads that were very fashionable at the time. I had previously thought they were pretty. Now, every time I see one of those bracelets, I see the bracelet covered in bits of torn infected skin and blood-soaked fur and I feel sick.

What horrible person could have done this to their cat and left it to suffer like this?

We never did find out. But at least this was a rescue and rehoming story to be proud of.

Although this turned out to be a bracelet, I have had to pick up cats and have watched surgeries of cats in very similar situations with their collars.

I remember one, Colin, who is still on the charity's website. The flea collar he must have had put on him as a kitten had managed to get around his stomach and it had gotten so tight, and been on him for so long, that it was barely visible where the skin had grown over it. There was only the occasional spot of blue visible between the bits of skin.

His was badly infected too and he would have died from that infection if he had not been found in time and brought into us. It was not clear what was wrong with him at first glance as the skin and fur had hidden the collar so well. It had to be dug out of him while he was under anaesthetic. Celia told me stories of cats having been killed when their collars had caught on tree branches too.

I realised that collars are a not a very good idea for cats. Cats are so prone to going missing, or moving out, or being left behind that they are better off without them really. A microchip will do just as good a job for their welfare.

Paddy

Paddy was another cat injured in a road accident. He was also in East Ham, as Linford had been, but not near the football ground. The people who called us had covered the big ginger tom cat with a blanket and positioned some rubbish bins around him to stop more cars from running him over, which was a rather odd sight to drive up to. They had correctly not wanted to move him but said that they had moved the bins to protect him as they had seen him run over by two different cars. Neither of which had stopped. I did not rate his survival chances.

I hoped he would not run. He was still in the middle of the road and not moving so I was worried it was already too late. I set up my basket next to him and asked if I could take the blanket with him. They were eager for me to do so to help keep him warm as they were clearly very worried about him, even though he was not their cat and they had not yet managed to work out who the owner was.

As I took hold of his scruff, he wriggled, showing me he was alive. His face was covered in blood. I gripped tighter in case he tried to run and wrapped the blanket further around him as I tucked an arm under him. I was able to lift him gently and horizontally into the basket (fortunately a top-opening basket), keeping him in the same position as much as possible. His legs were pawing slowly at the air and he made a horrible crying sound as I lifted him. Clearly in horrendous pain, he did not move any more than that.

His main injury turned out to be a broken jaw. He had lots of other smaller injuries but all those would heal on their own, so in theory at that point, he could survive. We did not however know what damage might have occurred to his brain as the car must have hit him in the head. The vets wired his jaw and cleaned him up and put him in intensive care on a drip.

I am still to this day filled with horror for having scruffed him when the pulling of the neck skin must have caused movement in his mouth which had caused him pain. That must have been why he cried so horribly. I did not have a choice as I could not risk him trying to run in that state. I know I did the right thing and yet I think I will always feel guilty.

He did not move much for a few days, but was showing signs of improvement, each day moving just a little bit more. He had to stay on the drip as he could not eat yet. A few days later, one of the nurses found him by his food bowl, he had dragged himself over to it, where they had left some special liquid food, but he was not able to eat by himself. But it was another sign of improvement and awareness. They started to syringe feed him the liquid food, bypassing the wires in his jaw. The nurses would sit in the intensive care ward with him on their laps, slowly and painstakingly giving him a few drops of food at a time, giving him time to swallow before adding any more. As he got stronger and his jaw started to heal, he had to have another operation to adjust the wire to make it easier for him to eat by himself. It took months and months of very intensive care before he could eat by himself again, and even then he had to have his food cut into very small pieces. He had clearly been a big cat but the few days on just a drip made him lose a lot of weight and it took a long time for him to regain it.

The people who had protected him called us for updates, and even came to see him, but they never did manage to find his owner.

As he healed, he would start to purr whilst being fed. We will never know what his personality was before, but with all the hands-on care, he came to love and appreciate any attention he could get, and he made sure everyone knew it. I visited him regularly once it was safe for me to say hello and stroke him without hurting him. At first, he would just purr but as he got more and more of his strength back, he would rub his face against my hand. Then later he would press his whole body against me and roll into my lap, cuddling up against me as tightly as possible. Once he was strong enough to walk again, he would come up to me and push his face against my face, as if he was giving me kisses.

He was almost immediately a favourite with the nurses, partly because he had been in such a sorry state that everyone felt protective of him, and partly because he was so cuddly. They nicknamed him Paddy.

He never was able to open his mouth fully again so was very lucky to be rehomed to a very dedicated cat-lover who could provide everything he needed, especially lots of cuddles. Paddy's adopter was already well-known by the nurses for the devotion she showed to her other disabled cats. Paddy came back often for cuddles… I mean check-ups.

The Fox at Piccadilly Circus

On the Saturday before Christmas, I was on call for the weekend. At around four in the afternoon, I got a call from one of our volunteers, Julie. There was a fox in a church with a severely injured leg and they had it 'sort of' cornered. We needed to get there fast to help them catch it.

Foxes are much more difficult to catch than cats, and I had never successfully caught one before. I borrowed Jon from the evening staff to come with me to help. On the drive, I had him call Si for advice. The address we were given turned out to be in central London, in Piccadilly Circus. The Friday rush hour traffic was horrendous. The streets were packed with people doing their Christmas shopping and out celebrating with workmates. Everyone was in a holiday mood and not paying all that much attention to the fact that they were walking in the road. I had to drive very slowly and carefully as people repeatedly walked in front of the van.

We got a trap out and were led up some stairs to see the most extraordinary sight. Halfway up, on a landing, a fox stood on three legs, against the wall, looking around frantically. Julie and one of the church workers were holding up a large, thick curtain across the stairs so that the fox could not see a way past to get down the stairs. They had been holding it up since before they called. They said their arms were aching terribly, but their determination to help the fox was heroic. At the top of the next set of stairs was a closed door. The banister was of wooden slats. The fox could fit through the gaps between these but would have had a long jump. He would also have been jumping into a crowd, as the church seemed to be hosting some sort of Christmas fair.

On closer inspection of the fox, there was a stump where one of its' front legs should have been that looked horrendously swollen and pus-covered.

I had little experience with foxes and certainly not when they were panicked. I never expected that we had a chance of catching this fox, but simultaneously, we did not have a choice. He would not be able to get past the crowds without hurting either himself, or a person, or probably both. The swollen leg was likely due to infection and so even if we could get him out of the church, he might die from that slowly and painfully. I had to work out a way to get him to a vet.

Between us, we carefully manoeuvred the curtain so that I could tuck the trap under it and through it, without leaving any gaps that the fox might try to run for. I moved everyone up a few steps, inch by inch. They were exhausted and relying on me to get the fox quickly but I still was not sure how it was going to react or the best way to catch it. I slowly managed to move the trap to face towards the fox in the hope that it would see the food inside. It was much too terrified to notice the food in the trap. I tried throwing little bits of chicken towards it. There was a moment where a piece of chicken landed near the fox, I was hoping it would smell it and look for food, but regrettably it scared the fox more and for a moment looked like the it might try to run through the gaps in the banister and jump into the crowd which had us all freeze with bated breath until it settled back against the wall.

I asked if we could get to the door at the top of the stairs, and sent Jon around to this to approach the fox to try to encourage it closer to us towards the trap, whilst we tried to hide ourselves behind the curtain. He went up with a dog catching rod, but we were reluctant to use this if it could be avoided.

As Jon approached, the fox started again looking around desperately for somewhere to run, but still would not go towards the trap, so Jon had to back off.

Jon suggested pushing the trap right into the corner, as far away from us as we could get it without panicking the fox. It took some manoeuvring as it was quite difficult to move the trap from behind the sheet without leaving any gaps. It seemed to notice the smallest spots of light and look as though it might bolt for them. I covered the trap with a thicker blanket, hoping that a dark place might look appealing to the fox, wondering if it might look like a safe den. We backed off again as far as we could go. Jon took a slow step towards the fox and this time it bolted into the trap.

Before I could close the trap, it had already curled itself up at the back, wrapping its tail over itself. I closed the trap and we covered it up fully and he looked much more relaxed despite our proximity to have a dark, enclosed space to hide in. Julie dropped the curtain with a sigh of relief, both for the fox's safety and for her sore arms. We had to squash through the dense crowds carrying the trap. No one paid attention to us to make room for us to get through, jostling us as they pushed through the crowds. I hoped they were bitten by fox fleas.

Back at the clinic, the on-call vet came in to have a look to see what we could do for the fox. The leg looked severely damaged. The vet and nurse anaesthetised him to have a closer look. Barely a stump was remaining of it. Perhaps it had been run over or it had been cut off in a trap. It looked like it had been missing for a while and was terribly infected.

At the clinic we did not have the type of cages suitable for treating foxes, and Celia tried to warn me that we would not get any help from any other fox charities. She did not explain why though. I was nevertheless absolutely determined to do whatever we could and spent a long time calling every fox charity in the South of England, asking for space, or help or even just advice.

They all told me the same thing. They advised me to either treat the fox (which would have involved amputating more of its leg and then putting it on a course of antibiotics until this was healed — impossible in the cages the charity used designed for domestic animals) and return him to the same place we had found him, or have him put to sleep.

They all explained that foxes cannot be relocated because they are so territorial that they will compete with another fox and one will end up killing the other. I tried to explain we could hardly return him to a church in busy Piccadilly Circus but they all insisted this was his only option. Even if they did take him in, they would ultimately return him there.

With one particularly helpful charity, all the way in Buckinghamshire, I discussed his survival chances at length. They explained that foxes use their front feet to pounce on their prey to immobilise them before killing them. No wonder the poor thing was so thin, he could not catch anything to eat. We could have tried to treat him and fatten him up at the clinic, but at some point, he would have to go back to fend for himself — which he clearly could not do. With the infection so far advanced, it was unlikely that he would make it anyway.

In an ideal world, with unlimited space, we would have built him a sanctuary to live for the rest of his life where he would be well cared for and have no competition. But this is not an ideal world. With heavy hearts we had to euthanize him. At least he would suffer no more.

Even though it was now very late in the day, Jon still had to catch upon all his work. Thankfully the volunteers had kindly stayed longer to ensure all the cats were fed and cleaned. I showed my appreciation by sweeping and mopping the clinic whilst he took the bins out. We had a running joke that I always seemed to need to walk across the clinic just as he had finished mopping, leaving footprints on the wet floor. Once everything was done and ready for the next day, we gathered in the office where Celia had bought us a takeaway meal. We talked through what had happened and consoled each other that we had done the best thing for the fox and that it was lucky he had been found so that he had not had to suffer a slow and painful death out there on his own in the cold December.

I love foxes and want them to eat, but I am much happier thinking that they are eating a sandwich from the back of a bakery, or a bowl of dog food from a fox-friendly neighbour, than either eating feral-born kittens or starving to death themselves.

Nichola Kirk

Rosie and the Adventure Playground

Whilst training Beth, a potential new rescue worker one day, I had a call out to a children's play area in Bethnal Green, where some kittens had been spotted living. We arrived expecting a standard children's play area but pulled up to a huge adventure playground, with massive multi-level wooden climbing frames.

The play area was currently closed for use. We were given the keys and agreed to lock up once we were done and post them into a nearby house. We were told the kittens were under a shed, but after looking around every shed-like structure, navigating around zip-lines, pirate-ship shaped playhouses and huge tyre-swings, we could not find them. I expected that I could have a great time playing there and wished I was there under nice circumstances. I spent many days afterwards noticing the tyre-swing and wanting to have a go.

We were on a time limit. The park would be reopening after the school holidays in only a couple of weeks, when noisy, hyperactive children would be running around everywhere, probably scaring the mother cat into moving her kittens to a new place. If they were not found in time, and she did move them, then they would grow up feral, if they survived at all. But cats are a patient species.

After sitting for a while quietly, we glimpsed three kittens playing inside a steel container. It was being used for storing children's bicycles and play equipment. We set up a blockage using a few cat baskets so they could not get out of the container and tried to get close enough to find where they were hiding. Unfortunately, after some investigating, I found a hole in the container floor, and no sign of them anywhere else inside. With no way of knowing how many kittens there were, and no way of accessing underneath the container, our only option was to set up a feeding pattern and to wait. The second day of doing this, we waited hours before we saw even a small sign of them. We had not expected to wait so long and had not brought lunch with us. Beth fetched us some food. It was rare that I had someone with me and I frequently survived on my stock of cereal bars or went hungry whenever I had to wait. I was grateful for the help and the company.

Eventually the same three kittens came out to the food. They were only about four weeks old, just old enough to start weaning and were barely showing any interest in the food at all. The mother cat later appeared from under the container. She was so wary that if she saw the slightest movement from our hiding place under a wooden bridge, she would bolt back under the container.

She was a tortoiseshell, with reddish markings, so we nicknamed her Rosie.

I have lot of sympathy for mother cats. I appreciate that it is difficult for people to comprehend how horrifying the whole experience is for them. When in season, they are chased, often by multiple males for days, barely being given a chance to sleep or eat.

Rosie was a particularly nervous cat. Beth and I soon learned not to move when she appeared and managed to stay still for long enough that she was tempted out to the food. The first time this happened, she was closely followed by a little black and white kitten that we had not seen earlier. This meant there were at least four kittens.

While she ate, the kitten stood underneath her suckling from her, but showing no interest whatsoever in the kitten food.

Although the playground was large enough all by itself to feel like a little patch of safety, it was surrounded by busy

London roads and would be very dangerous for the kittens once they started to venture out.

The following day, we repeated the process of setting up the trap and putting food down, then went back to our hiding place under the bridge and settled down to wait. The three original kittens came out to play, using the trap as a toy, climbing over it and batting at bits of strong dangling from it. Later the mother appeared, this time from the gate. She ate from the trap before leading the kittens under the container to feed them. We kept going at a similar time each day and the same three kittens started to get into the routine and came out quite quickly after we arrived. They started to take an interest in the food and would have a few bites but only the same three came out — never the black and white one.

Each day we had to report back to Celia that we had not been able to catch them because we could not leave that one behind. She repeatedly asked me if I was sure that there had been a black and white one in the first place. She made me doubt myself, but I was so sure... she chose to trust me, letting me wait for it.

I started to worry that something bad had happened to it, or that Rosie had already moved it elsewhere — but then would not she have also moved the others?

The three grew in confidence each day and soon were clambering up the nearby children's climbing wall and chasing each other around happily. But we needed to catch them before the playground reopened, and before they became fully feral.

The debate began between me and Celia about the chance of the fourth kitten still being alive. I was insistent that he was still there and reluctant to catch the family until he appeared or we had literally no more time before the park reopened. I could not face the possibility that he might not be alive, even though he had seemed much smaller and weaker than his siblings on that one time that I had seen him.

I borrowed a motion-sensor night-vision camera from Si to set up in the playground to watch a plate of food overnight, only two nights before they had to be caught, in the hope of finding out once and for all if the little black and white one was still around. We had images of all the others, and a large ginger tom too, but no sign of the little black and white. The park keepers were becoming increasingly agitated with the how long we were taking. Just as I was becoming increasingly frustrated with the impossibility of the situation — how could I take away the family, without being sure that we had all of them?

All evidence suggested that it was too late for the black and white one. I arranged for a foster home to be ready to receive the feral family and went to catch them. I took along Beth to show her how to trap in a mum and kitten situation. I explained that in the event that all of the family would not go into the trap at the same time, we would try to trap the kittens first, and then trap the mother separately, using the kittens as bait if food alone would not tempt her. We would have to have all the kittens in the trap at the same time before catching them as they would not be likely to re-enter if they saw the others being caught. The mother would also have to not be present. We had to act now as if for any reason we could not catch them, we would need the following, and final, day to do so.

Although the three kittens went into the trap as usual there was no sign of Rosie, and I could not risk taking them without her, because without the kittens, she might move out and disappear, only to become pregnant again within weeks, or even days, and soon be in the same situation elsewhere.

I waited for so long in the hope that she would turn up, that someone had locked the outer gate, trapping us inside. We had to climb a four-foot fence, easy enough without all the equipment, but I could not have managed lifting over all the heavy traps on my own so was pleased to have someone with me.

It was then only the day before the park was to open. We were out of time, they would have to be caught today. I returned with various plans in mind;

Plan A: catch the three, then Rosie and leave food for a few days in case the fourth kitten did turn out to still be alive;

Plan B: catch the three without the mother and come back for her, trapping from the street if necessary;

Plan C (and worst case scenario): catch whoever I could and hope for the best.

I would have to play it by ear and adapt my methods to get as many as possible out of there. We set up and went to our usual hiding place. Soon after, the three kittens came out, by now well versed in the feeding routine.

But this time, finally, out came the little black and white kitten too.

What if he would not go in the trap at the same time as the others? Would I be able to catch him separately? Would he go in the trap at all? The kittens played with the trap and in the grass for a short while, putting their paws through the bars of the trap, teasing me to make me think they were not going to go in the trap at all that day.

Eventually one little ginger kitten went in and started eating, closely followed by another ginger kitten and the black and white one. I tensed up, ready to catch them if possible, and safe to do so without the fourth kitten seeing.

The fourth, a tabby, carried on playing with the long grass for another minute, enhancing my tension, before giving in to temptation and going in. As soon as it was far enough inside, I closed the trap. The poor little babies were very scared and ran up the walls of the trap, I covered them as quickly as I could get there to calm them, then immediately transferred them into a carrier, with the help of my colleague, and moved them out the way so I could set the trap back up. They calmed down as soon as they were in the carrier and huddled together in the corner. Just as I had finished this, Rosie appeared, entering the park under the gate.

She would not go straight up to the container, thankfully giving me time to hurriedly get everything set back up for her and get myself back into hiding. She went around behind us to the opposite side of the playground. I was so tense with worry that my whole body started to ache. Rosie sniffed around the boundaries of what she must have considered her territory, presumably to make sure there were no cat intruders. She started making her way towards the trap whilst sniffing at every corner of the park, and, it felt like, every strand of grass. Instead of going to the food, she went straight underneath the container. She must have been suspicious because she could not see her kittens out playing as usual. I worried that she would realise that her kittens were missing and go in search of them instead of going to eat. This would mean that we would have to set them up as bait, which I was always reluctant to do unless absolutely necessary as it would be stressful both for her and the kittens who would have to be slightly uncovered and so more prone to fear. But then she appeared again and walked straight into the trap. I snapped the trap shut quickly and we covered it and locked it tightly. Then we collapsed laughing with relief.

We did leave food there, just in case there might be a fifth kitten, and had the park staff carry this on for a few more days to be doubly certain, but there were no more.

Rosie and her kittens went into a foster home where they had a whole room to themselves, rather than a cage. Rosie's kittens were easily tamed in their foster home and even the mother calmed down enough that she was later able to be homed to a couple that were happy to give a loving home to a nervous cat.

A nice surprise

One of our volunteers alerted us to a cat with a severely swollen paw that she had been feeding. The tom cat had been injured since the night before, but she had not been able to get hold of him. The cat did not turn up at his usual feeding time, but I could not leave in case he turned up the moment I left.

I hid inside the house by the patio door and I had to pull a curtain half across me because the sun was shining so strongly I could feel my pale skin burning. The food in the trap went dry quickly in the heat. I changed the food in the trap for fresh food and put the old food next to me where I was hiding, to be put in the bin later. Not long after I had done this, the cat with the swollen paw finally turned up, but walked straight past the trap and ignores the food completely. This had me rather worried as he was limping really badly, and I feared that perhaps he is so distracted by his injury that he does not feel like eating. This would have made him impossible to catch as I had been told that he was very, very nervous.

He limped over in my direction and peered inside the house, then waited by the back door for a minute. I wondered if he was used to a routine where they bring the food out to him. I moved the curtain and moved towards him but he backed off, so I stopped and inched back out of his view.

He then came forward again, walking straight past me to eat the old food that was right next to me. I did not want him to eat much of this as if he ate too much, he would not be hungry enough to go in the trap, but I did not want to scare him off completely so I thought that perhaps, if he is prepared to come this close to me, I might be able to get a hand on him, and if not, at least I can take away the dry food so that he did not fill up on it.

I moved slowly towards him, and got a basket ready nearby. He was a little nervous at first, and backed away, but he wanted the food enough to come back and while he was eating, I inched closer and was able to gently stroked his head and down his back to his neck. He did not back away again so I stroked him again then held him tightly by the scruff of his neck and lifted him into the basket, lowering him carefully so as not to hurt his paw.

I could barely believe after all that time waiting for him, expecting to have to trap him, and expecting a feral cat, I had managed to pick him up so easily. Of course, it was easier for me to get cats into baskets than it was for other people, even experienced volunteers. I had learned how to move so as not to scare them and was confident in my ability to scruff a cat quickly and securely, which was not a skill that many people have to learn.

Once we got back to the clinic, the vet found a bad bite wound through his paw that had become badly infected and had swollen to twice the size, so he was given pain relief and antibiotics. After this, the cat appeared completely tame. We wondered where his owner was, but by his usual nervousness and the fact he had not been taken to a vet after twenty four hours with this injury, as well as his not being neutered or micro-chipped, we assume he is a typical 'pre-loved' cat, whose owners had moved away leaving him behind.

Sana happily took him back once he was recovered and he was allowed into her house as and when he wished from then on, even sleeping on her bed.

Yin Yang

I arrived in Stepney to collect a pregnant, black cat from a family who were moving home the following day. The cat was a little nervous of strangers so had to be coaxed with food to come close enough for me to pick her up. Once she was in the van and I asked for the paperwork to be signed, I noticed a white cat, also pregnant, and asked what was to happen with her. They then revealed that another family member was able to take her on and then asked if the charity would help rehome the kittens.

I asked whether that person could perhaps take the other cat too, and they explained that it was their gran and she could only manage one with a litter. I wanted to know why they had let the cats get pregnant in the first place. They explained that they had wanted the children to play with the kittens. They had chosen to keep the white cat over the black one because, 'She is white, so her kittens will be cute and we want to play with them!'

Why on Earth would they want her to have kittens when they had no intention of keeping them themselves? Had it not occurred to them that those poor cats had to go through a pregnancy, and birth and raise their litter only to have them all taken away?

I told them about the dozens of extremely cute kittens in our foster homes and explained that it is unfair of them to allow their cats to have kittens when so many others are desperately seeking good homes. If they wanted to play with kittens, but did not want to keep the kittens, why not foster a litter instead? I explained that I would not agree to help them with the kittens without a definite agreement that they would get the mother neutered immediately after, as otherwise they would just do the same thing again with no consequences for them. I was reluctant to agree to help them at all to home the kittens as they had made the conscious decision to let their cat get pregnant and by homing their kittens through the charity, one less litter could be rescued from the streets. The family would not promise to get the white cat neutered and I was very tempted to give them their pregnant black cat back too to make them sort out their own mess rather than expecting a charity to do it for them. I did not do this though, mostly because I would feel too sorry for the black cat going back to a life of producing endless kittens to be used as toys. Celia called them later and convinced them to get all their adults neutered, they agreed to on condition that the charity rehomed their kittens, which seemed like a fair compromise to prevent future unwanted kittens.

Teamwork

In response to a call from a popular dog charity, I visited a lady in Hackney who had multiple cats that kept breeding. Initially I was not given any more information and there was no answer at the door, so I posted a note offering to help her with neutering her cats. She called me back later the same day and explained that she was feeding four female strays, but she had been struggling to keep up with the number of kittens they kept having. She could not afford to have them neutered. We arranged for them to be collected and neutered and for us to arrange help with the cost, which we could do either through the charity's Neuter Return scheme or through Cats Protection's stray neutering vouchers. The feeder was not home for any length of time until the following Tuesday, so I offered to pick them up Tuesday morning for neutering the same day and to drop them off Tuesday evening so that they would not be away from their kittens for long. She was so relieved to have a solution, and was happy to find homes for the kittens herself, ensuring that they too would be neutered when old enough. I loved meeting such caring people as this person, who genuinely want to help, and have discovered first-hand how quickly cats breed, so appreciate what the charity is up against.

Cemetery 1

I had never expected, intended or desired to spend a night in a cemetery. This story is about the first time that I experienced one for the good of cat-kind.

The clinic had a call in the day about six kittens running loose in the cemetery only five minutes away from the charity in East Ham. We hurried there only to find that the staff had already caught five of the six kittens and put them in a box in the office. We asked where the sixth kitten was. They said, 'Not to worry, we will find him later.' We were not impressed by this. Using our method of catching cats, we would have had all six easily, with no escapees, as they would have been lured, not chased.

They then explained that they had potential homes for at least three of the kittens already.

One of the biggest issues I struggled with while working in animal rescue is that it is all a matter of opinion. It was my opinion that these people barely needed to call us at all. They were so close to having dealt with the situation themselves.

It was Si and Celia's (over the phone) opinion that the staff should not have tried to catch the kittens at all as they had only made it more difficult for us by scaring the last kitten so much that it had gone into hiding.

In the cemetery, Si and I transferred the five kittens into a secure carrier, out of the cardboard box, as desperate kittens can scratch through cardboard in seconds. We took all five back to the clinic as they all had fleas and we wanted to check them over. We asked the people to come pick up the ones they had homes for later from the clinic, and we did the home-check the same day to make sure they were going to good homes.

We then set up traps in different areas of the cemetery around where the kittens had last been and waited in our vans.

Eventually Si had to leave. I re-positioned myself more centrally and hoped that the kitten would come out before dark. I had never been alone in a cemetery before, never mind at night.

As the sun was going down, all sorts of terrifying thoughts crossed my mind. I could not decide whether I believed in ghosts, but I had watched far too many scary films. No one arrived to distract me, and I started to see shapes in the dusk. I called Pete, desperate for him to hurry and thankfully he turned up just before it got completely dark.

The staff locked us in. I was partly worried about being locked in with the ghosts, but I was simultaneously pleased that at least it would be nice and quiet, making the kitten more likely to emerge.

We had to be quiet for over an hour before the kitten finally appeared. He crept out from under a flat gravestone slab not too far from where I had set the trap. He was not interested in food though. The poor boy started to cry, mewing pitifully. He ran all around the graveyard and back again, looking for his mother and his siblings, crying to them. He sounded so sad. He did this for hours and showed no interest at all in going in the trap, no matter where I put it or what food was in or near it. In the end, the staff could not wait any longer to let us out before they went to bed and asked us to leave.

The next day I went back as early as I could get in. It was a lovely sunny day and I was prepared with sardines and hot chicken. How could he possibly resist after a night with no food? I set up the trap next to the grave he had been hiding under with the hot chicken first. He did not come out. I added the sardines. He still did not come out. I stayed there the whole day. There were a few people around but no one disturbed me or the spot where I suspected the kitten must be back in hiding.

It started to get dark again and the graveyard went silent. He still did not come out. I was not even sure he was there, so I asked one of the staff, just before they left, if they could help me check under the gravestone to see if he could feel anything. I had not dared due to fear of touching something I would never get over. He explained to me that burials are very deep and that graves often fall in slightly over time, leaving a slight gap under the slab, but that there was nothing there that could hurt (or worry) me, except perhaps a terrified kitten. He felt underneath with a glove - for fear of being scratched - but could not feel a kitten.

Once he had gone, I summoned up the courage to try too. Without a glove I might have been able to feel fur. But I had no luck either. The staff had offered to get help to lift the stone, but I pointed out that it would not help because the kitten would just run to a new hiding place faster than we would be able to catch him in such an open space. Even though they had gotten lucky catching the others, this kitten was clearly too fast, too smart and too scared.

It was even darker this time before Pete said he was on his way. I had an idea before he set off and asked him to bring one of this kittens' siblings. He did, and we put him in a carrier behind the trap. We made him as comfortable as we could with blankets and snacks and settled in to wait.

Once it was fully dark, the ginger kitten appeared from under the same slab as last time. Clearly he had a good, deep hiding spot. He ran around quietly at first, but soon started to cry again. Unfortunately, he did not know that we were there to help him and all he had to do was come to us and we would take him to his family. Or at least to his siblings. I hoped that the owner who had dumped the kittens would think to get their cat neutered before she got pregnant again. It only cost £20 at the time; hardly expensive.

The ginger kitten again ignored the food completely. As he came closer to us, crying, the kitten in the carrier heard him and started to mew back to him. This made him frantic as he could not pinpoint it at first. Most kittens would have found the other kitten in minutes, or seconds even but he was too distressed to concentrate. He ran around more quickly, getting further away and then closer, all the time crying in an even higher pitch. It was heart-breaking to hear, but it was for his own good as it might be the only way we could catch him.

The kitten in the carrier almost sounded like he was offering comfort. It seemed to me as though the ginger was saying, 'Where are you?' and his brother was saying, 'It's ok, I'm right here'.

The ginger kitten had repeatedly climbed a particularly tall gravestone with an angel on top to get a better view. When he next moved away to search at the far end of the graveyard, Pete helped me move the trap, and the kitten in his carrier, to be next to the angel. This time when he came back and climbed the angel statue, he could hear his brother better and he got very excited.

He climbed down and started sniffing around the trap, finally noticing it. He could not figure out the way in because he wanted to go in through the back as that was where his brother was.

The staff started heading towards us to tell us it was late and that we would need to leave. But he was walking around the trap trying to find away in! As they got closer, I put my finger on my lips, in the hope they would notice and realise the kitten was there and not come any closer. They understood and paused, watching.

He found the entrance and bounded happily along the trap to where he could now see his brother. I closed it quickly and we all cheered. Back at the clinic he was so happy to be reunited with the rest of his little family.

Cat Rescuer

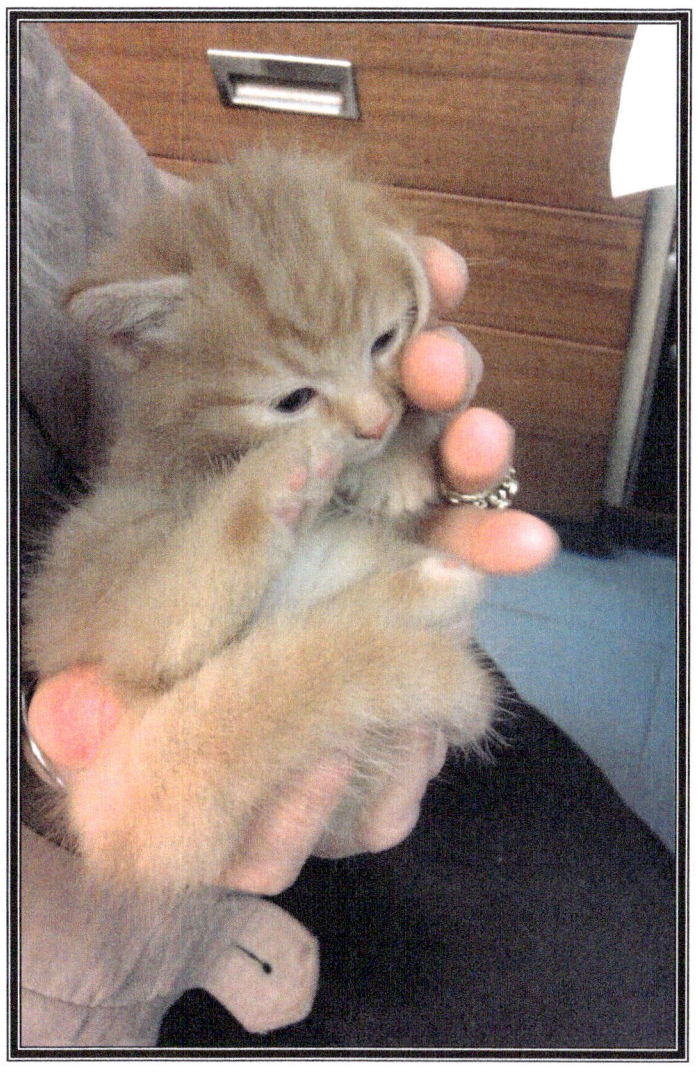

Tintin

It was a very long time before I ever even saw Tintin after I first heard about him. It must have been at least a month, probably more. I was called out to rescue the injured cat. I spoke to a few different people in the neighbourhood who had seen him raiding their bins and had seen him hurt various times in the past. They said he had always healed which was why no one had called before. But that this wound seemed to be getting worse rather than better. No one was sure who fed him, although pointed out people that they thought might be doing so. That first day I could not find the cat, or anyone who fed him, despite them all claiming to know of him and worry about him.

I left some food with the person who had called us and asked her to feed him once a day, at the same time every day until he had developed a routine so that I could come and trap him. There was no way I would be able to do so when he turned up at random times and at no specific place. She agreed to do this. If he was not being fed, and was really eating out of bins, he should be turning up ready and waiting for the food within only a couple of days.

I called her a week later as I had not heard from her. She said she had not been feeding him as she did not want him to become reliant on her. I expressed again my intention to trap him and bring him into the clinic. She agreed again to feed him.

A few days later, I checked again, and she had another excuse for why she still was not feeding him. I closed my eyes, counted to ten and tried to control my frustration. I did not know what to do next, short of going and feeding him every day myself but it was quite far away from the clinic.

I enlisted help from Si. If anyone could convince her to feed the cat, he could. He would probably tell her something about finding him dead on her doorstep in the morning. Or

Cat Rescuer

about how he would start bringing flies to her house as he walked past with an infected injury, or something else horrific and guaranteed to scare her into feeding the cat.

If that failed, I really would go every day and put food down myself.

I gave Si a 'tour' of the pretty street with big, fancy houses. I pointed out where the cat had been seen, and by whom, who I had been told fed him, and who had denied ever having fed him. We looked around for a couple of hours and put down chicken and warm, buttered kippers in a bowl in case the cat turned up.

Just as we were about to leave, a car pulled into a house opposite. I had not spoken to the drivers before because they had not previously been home and so we headed over to introduce ourselves. They had their own cat, and knew of the stray, and had been feeling really sorry for him, but had not known how to help. We asked them if they would set up a feeding pattern, and they were more than willing. They were so happy to be able to help that they even declined our food and insisted on feeding him with their own.

Two weeks later, they had coaxed him into such a good routine that he was ready to be trapped. We had not been able to leave a dummy trap because it was a front garden and it was not safe to do so. They had been feeding in the morning, so Si took over the job. He expected to have to go a few days in a row to get the cat used to the trap first before he would go in. When he arrived, the cat was already eagerly waiting for his breakfast on the doorstep. Si set up the trap while the cat backed off to a distance and watched him. Si expected him to be wary of him, the trap and the changes. But the moment he turned his back, Si barely had time to get himself in a position to close it before the cat walked straight into the trap.

I therefore first met Tintin back at the clinic, more than three weeks after I had heard of him. I did not know what sort of injury to expect, but nothing could have prepared me for the state he was in. I have never seen a worse injury on a living cat. Something had clearly cut across the top of his head. The shape of the cut looked suspiciously like the sharp edge of a tin as he could have put his head in one whilst trying to find food for himself in a bin, because no one would feed him, and gotten caught and cut his head trying to get himself out. Louise therefore named him Tintin rather unflatteringly. The wound had gotten infected, worsened and widened until there was barely any skin left on the top of his head. As the wound had tried to heal itself, it had tugged up the skin of his eyelids into an odd clown like expression.

He had to be kept scrupulously clean whilst the wound healed. It was such a large open wound that the nurses had to be very careful to prevent infection. No one could visit him except the on-duty nurse, who would have to disinfect themselves thoroughly first. He was having drops put in his eyes every couple of hours, day and night, because he still could not blink properly as the skin was too tight to give his eyelid sufficient movement. He had to have multiple skin grafts. When I saw him on the table having the grafts done, his freaky eyelid was still lifted oddly, even asleep.

After he had been with us for a few months, I was helping to feed the cats one evening when a nurse invited me in to see Tintin, saying he was past the worst of the risk of infection. He was loose in the intensive care room while the nurse cleaned him out.

He was a lovely fluffy silver colour with bits of white. He still had stitches in a circle on the top of his head, looking as if he had recently had brain surgery, or like Frankenstein's monster. Fur had grown (albeit much shorter than on the rest of him) from all the skin grafts on top of his head, so it stuck out oddly in random directions. I sat down on the floor near him. I really was not sure how friendly he was going to be but knew he was at least tame. His eyes were still pulled up at the corners, much less than they been, but he still looked kind of grotesque. I crouched down and offered him my hand to sniff. He pressed his head against my hand and rubbed against it. I could feel his stitches as he rubbed, the felt rough and spiky. If they were uncomfortable for me to just touch them, they must have been very uncomfortable for him. They must have been itching him because he rubbed against my hand, using me to scratch himself. I could not stroke him fast enough for his liking, I had to alternate hands quickly to keep him satisfied.

Even after more skin grafts, he never quite looked normal, but he was such a sweet, loveable cat that someone eventually fell in love with him and gave him his forever home where he would never have to scavenge again.

Terry

Terry asked the charity for help when his cat situation got out of hand. He had six females, seven males and fifteen kittens.

The story unravelled that he had taken in a stray cat a few years ago and started to feed her. She had promptly moved in with him and given birth in his home. He fell in love with her kittens and kindly took all of those on too, rather than trying to rehome them. He lived in a converted warehouse so had plenty of room. The warehouse was in the middle of a circle of terraced buildings in Hackney, with only one exit to the road, making it relatively safe from traffic.

He was against neutering and did not realise how quickly cats reproduce. Not long after, his stray gave birth again, and he kept the whole litter again, although feeding them was getting expensive. Then winter arrived. His first cat did not have any more kittens for a while, and he thought it would be ok. The little ones grew up in his care.

He talked to them all in a soft, soothing voice. He enjoyed teaching them to play and hunt. He rearranged his whole home for them, with hiding places and places for them to climb and jump across. It was quite amazing. The warehouse where he cared for them was also his workplace, he made things with sheets of metal. That area was quite a dangerous place for kittens really, but he moved the machinery and metal into the safest possible arrangement to protect them. Although some accidents did happen unfortunately, and he told me how devastated he had been when his first cat had knocked a table over onto herself and been killed. He was still grieving for her. It certainly made him extra careful in being sure everything was extra-safe from then on.

Those kittens grew up the most loved of any. He absolutely doted on them. He fed them real meat. Not tinned food from a supermarket but meat from the butchers. They seemed to eat better than him. He explained to me that he had been in a dark place in his life when the first cat had turned up, and she had saved him from his own unhappiness and had given him something to live for. She was like a daughter to him and he had felt like a granddaddy when she had given birth, making him feel special and needed, and helping him suppress unhappy thoughts.

The following summer though, the female kittens were all grown up and most of them gave birth within days of each other. One had unfortunately miscarried, which had then led to getting mastitis (an infection in the mammary glands) and she had been treated at C.H.A.T. Unfortunately, it was too late for her. The infection had turned into septicaemia (an infection in the bloodstream) and there was nothing that the vets could do to save her. Terry had been devastated and stayed with her in her last moments, and long after, holding her to comfort her as she passed.

He had agreed to allow Celia to neuter his girls. But for one reason or another, not all of them were done. Perhaps more care should have been taken on the charity's part, but I do not think anyone at the time realised that Terry would not ensure that the neutering was complete. Perhaps he allowed all the adults to be neutered, but then never got around to neutering their kittens the following year before they all fell pregnant. I found out first-hand that Terry was always so busy himself that it was difficult to pin down a time when he could even meet me, never mind have brought cats to the charity to be neutered. It was not his priority. He had to work. Although I really believe it should be everyone's priority if they take on a cat. If necessary, even to take a day off work to ensure that their pet gets to the vet to be checked and neutered before it is let outside.

Terry did not help himself. But in his case, it was not laziness, or ignorance. I sympathised completely with him. When you are fighting depression, anything that can save you from that misery must be nurtured. But not at the expense of another's happiness or safety.

Once Terry's cats had started to suffer, once there were so many that the flu was prevalent, once there were too many to afford to feed the butcher's meats, or even the cheapest cat biscuit, he finally accepted that it was time to take neutering seriously. Many of the cats over the years had gone missing, Terry presumed that they had either moved in with other people or managed to get out into the road and been killed.

My agreement with Terry was that we would neuter, then return as many as he felt he could manage (the thirteen adults) and rehome any others (the fifteen kittens).

I attended to pick up two of the mother cats with older kittens, who would be returned the same day so that they could continue feeding their kittens. Mother cats can get pregnant again briefly when their kittens are two weeks old, and then again anytime from when their kittens are six weeks old, so we did not want to leave them.

He wanted to raise and socialise the kittens himself first, until they were old enough to be rehomed, which we were happy with as long as they did not get flu and were safe. He promised to keep them all in the indoor area, and even blocked off a few cat doors to make sure they could not get out when he was not looking. There was one litter under a chair, one by the bed, one behind the TV and one in the kitchen cupboard. He had left them where the mothers had birthed them but put blankets under them to keep them cosy and warm. He handled each one every day. I checked them all for signs of flu, but all looked healthy. He did not know exactly where the fifth litter had been born as their mother was the most nervous of them all and had not had them inside the building. He suspected that she might have had them in another building, but we could not find them. They were likely to have been in a shed of one of the surrounding houses.

The mother cats had been raised with only Terry for human company and although perfectly friendly with him, acted as good as feral towards me. The first time I went, we planned for him to lock them in one room, where I could catch them or would be able to encourage them to run into somewhere I could scruff them. Except that when I came to do this, the 'room' that he had trapped them in was the whole warehouse, sectioned off into a makeshift home, but without walls to stop a cat. The bedroom consisted of a homemade, spiral staircase up to a huge piece of wood in the rafters with his bed on it.

This resulted in rather a wild and distressing chase to catch the first two females as Terry did not want me to use the trap, and he could not bear to put them into baskets himself. I think he thought it would be too scary for his girls. Or maybe he just thought they would be easier to catch than they were.

They would run to the door and jump up at the handle, then to their locked catflap, trying to push through. Then, when we got close, they would run to the opposite side of the room, via a cupboard or under the chairs so we could not reach them or corner them, and climb the ladder, or jump up onto tall furniture. After we went around in circles a few times like this, Terry himself did end up catching both, which I wished I had insisted upon from the start.

I was really upset by the whole experience myself and vowed never to let anyone again convince me to hand-catch a cat that was better off trapped. Trapping is not as scary as it sounds. Fair enough, they are often alarmed when the trap first snaps shut, but once a sheet is put over the cage, they calm down very quickly. Whereas a mad chase round the room caused them panic for the duration, and they continued to pant in fear for a long while afterwards.

A couple of weeks after Terry's first two cats went home, more of the kittens were old enough to spend a few hours alone while the mothers were neutered.

Terry had bought himself a carrier and managed to bring two of them in. One only had two kittens and had not been looking after them much recently, so he brought them in as well for a check-up.

The vets discovered that the mother cat, Charlotte, had mastitis. We thought that perhaps she might have had a genetic predisposition to it, as it had been her 'aunt' who had passed away from the same condition. Her breasts were swollen, red and clearly very sore. Charlotte's kittens were taken away from her temporarily as they kept trying to feed from her and it had become too painful for her. They were hand-fed by Iris in reception, who returned them to Charlotte when they would be least hungry, a couple of times a day so that they could all cuddle up together. Charlotte was put on strong antibiotics, but the infection seemed to keep getting worse. She became very weak and the skin started to turn bright red and peel off. The nurses feared for her life and Terry was distraught.

Celia insisted that if she was neutered, she would have less hormones to affect the mastitis and it would help her heal. The vets were sceptical of this but agreed to give it a try. After Charlotte was neutered, plus a lot of hard work and TLC, she did gradually recover. She ate a little more each day and eventually was strong enough to go home. It took a couple of weeks for all this and the kittens were almost old enough to be rehomed, eating mostly solid food, so stayed at the clinic and were rehomed shortly. Terry had to continue to keep Charlotte clean and rub in cream to help her skin heal the last little bit.

We ended up neutering all seven of Terry's males, and five of the females, and rehomed the kittens of those five.

The sixth mother was the one who had given birth out of the living area in an unknown location.

A few months later, I eventually caught the sixth mother along with two of her kittens (feral by this point of course). This was after Terry called us to say that she had three kittens, and the third had been missing for days (never having told us that they had turned up at all).

Terry suspected that the kitten had managed to climb over a wall and could not get back. He looked in all the surrounding gardens, getting permission from all the neighbours, and set up a ladder on the other side of the wall to help her get back up. He put fresh food on top of the wall every day.

Before the last kitten had been caught, Terry revealed that he was being evicted. I leafleted the whole block, and even a couple of neighbouring blocks twice to try locate the missing kitten in time but no one had even seen it. We worried that once Terry was gone, it would not have anyone to feed it. But at the same time, if it was not coming to him for food, it must have somewhere else to eat already. Another worry was that Sod's Law meant that it would surely be female.

Whilst leafleting the second time, I discovered a lady named Julie. She rushed out after I posted the leaflet and invited me in. She had not seen the little black kitten that I was after but was knee deep in stray cats that she had taken in to care for. Julie turned out to be the reason that Terry had not been overrun by kittens' years before. Terry had been completely oblivious to the impact he was having around him while unconsciously breeding his cats. Julie had not even realised that the cats had someone else looking after them as they were so nervous.

She had been systematically catching, taming, neutering and rehoming the cats for years. She had a house full of cats that she was trying to tame sufficiently to rehome. She had one cat that had a broken leg that had been to the vet for surgery and was recovering. She used her own money for all of them and must have spent thousands, battling against the constant flow of more and more cats and kittens. She agreed to keep an eye out for the kitten and we offered to help with any that she needed help with.

Terry took the rest of the cats with him and kept them indoors for a few weeks until he was sure they had made themselves at home and would not get lost.

Even after Terry's eviction, still the black kitten did not turn up. We had been putting food down in the warehouse until the landlord changed the locks to the gate. Then we pushed food under the gate instead.

One night Celia came with me. We spotted a black cat, who I was certain was too big to be the kitten, but who Celia insisted we catch. We spent a whole evening in the van, with the trap ready, and did catch it. We took it in for neutering, but it turned out to be an adult male, too old to be the one we were looking for.

We put up posters to see if we had inadvertently stolen someone's cat and someone did call us about him. It turned out that he was a stray, but one that the couple liked very much. Once they heard he was neutered, and that no one else had contacted us about him, they decided that they would like to keep him so they came and picked him up and took him home forever, even paying his bill, although we did not ask them to.

It was another two months later when a smaller black cat turned up at the house of the same couple. They knew we were looking for a similar cat so they fed it for a few days to get it to keep coming back, then I went with my trap to get it. The boy that they had taken in previously was there and seemed very happy with his new home. He trotted over to me confidently rubbing against me to ask for a stroke.

He accepted a few treats from me then ran off down the garden, only to return minutes later with the little black cat in tow. He appeared to have adopted her, and she had attached on to him for company. He led her to the food and she, trusting him completely, walked in the trap. We took her in for neutering and rehoming. She was indeed a female, and she was about the right age to be the kitten we were looking for, but luckily had not yet gotten pregnant. The next day, the couple called to say that their boy had become so distressed without her that they would like to adopt her too. They picked her up and kept her in their spare room with him for a week while she recovered from her operation, and while they tamed her. This did not take very long at all as she would go wherever their boy went, and trust whomever he trusted. It was a very sweet ending to a very long, frustrating job.

Nichola Kirk

Catflap

Another time I got caught out when my instructions were not followed, causing panicked cats to fly around a room, was when trying to catch a mother cat and four five-month-old kittens. I told a woman that I would be using the trap in her kitchen. I explained that she must not close the cat flap or I would not be able to trap the four kittens that were in there because they would panic. She closed the catflap.

The cats flew in every direction once they realised they could not leave by their usual route and half her kitchen got smashed. There were plant pots and tea pots and all sorts of broken crockery all over the floor. The woman was waving her arms in the air, chasing the cats around the tiny kitchen, flustered and shouting. I made an excuse to get her to leave the room, 'to fetch some more treats.' To get her out of the way.

I positioned a carrier against the door to effectively lock her out and told her she could not come back in because I was trying to get one of the kittens from behind the door and I did not want it to escape into the rest of the house. I'm not a fan of lying, but I was not going to let her cause any more stress to those poor kittens with her flailing and yelling.

I sat quietly for a few minutes, to give the kitten's time to calm down. Positioning the trap in front of the catflap, I added food inside and a sheet over the top. I left it open at the back, so that the cats would be able to see the catflap. I could only see one of the cats so I moved towards him where he was cowering on the worktop. He manoeuvred around me and ran straight into the trap. I put in a divider to close off the back half of the trap to shut him in there whilst leaving space for another.

I approached another kitten, who was barely hidden behind the bread bin. That one did exactly the same thing. I closed him in the front half, then lifted the divider to let him in the part with his sibling, so that I could open the front half again.

I searched everywhere for the next two, even looking in the cupboards. I then waited quietly to listen and think about where I had not looked. Then I spotted a little bit of ginger fur revealing the third kitten. He had managed to squash himself into a gap between the wall and a wall-mounted boiler. Somehow getting himself so squashed in that he was managing to hold himself, almost suspended in the air, as there was nothing below him to stand on.

I tried to scruff him out, but could barely get my hand in. Instead, I positioned a carrier upright underneath him, and pushed him down into it, conscientiously slowly as he tried to hang on, scraping his claws against the wall. I put a lid over the basket and transferred him into the trap with his two siblings.

I got down on my hand and knees and went over every inch of space that a cat could hide. The fourth kitten was not in there. I went out to the woman, who had a look around the rest of the house. She found the kitten in an upstairs bedroom, and chased him down into the kitchen, where he ran straight into the trap too.

It had been so easy once I had calmed them down that I knew I would have been able to get them in the trap all even more easily if she had not closed the cat flap. Yes, they would have left while I set up, but they would have come straight back in once they thought I had left.

I still had to catch the mother, who was outside. She was supposed to be much friendlier than her kittens, likely the victim of being left behind when her owner moved away, leaving her stray and without a home to take her kittens to be tamed in. She was obviously still going to be wary of a stranger. I advised the woman that we probably would not get the mother cat that same day, especially if she had heard the noise, but I would at least like to try to meet her.

The woman made us both a cup of tea to settle our nerves. Despite my having turned on my calm self outwardly, I was still shaking from the stress and adrenalin. While she brewed the tea, and had her back turned, I spotted a nose sniffing through the now unlocked cat flap.

I had a feeling that the woman was going to overreact again, scaring the cat away. I repositioned myself, squatting near the cat-flap, in a way that would prevent the woman from seeing the cat until she was all the way in the room. I did not look towards the mother cat but kept her in my peripheral vision, with the open carrier next to me and the food beside it. The cat came in very slowly and cautiously, until she spotted the tuna on her plate. Then she jumped the rest of the way through into the kitchen and tucked into the food, right next to me. She was a very pretty, longhaired tortoiseshell. The lady turned around to me just at that moment, saw her and exclaimed, 'She's here!'

Bad timing - the cat heard and promptly ran back outside. I asked the woman to continue making the tea and to not move any more than necessary and to not speak. She stayed quiet but her eyes were wide with anxiety.

The cat clearly loved her tuna and came back inside within a minute.

I moved my hand next to the bowl. She carried on eating.

I stroked the back of my hand against her. She flinched.

I stroked along her back, once, twice, scruffed.

As I lifted her into the carrier, I tucked her back legs and tail up to hold her weight with my other arm and she complacently tucked herself into a ball, just like a newborn kitten does when carried by its mother. It makes my heart swell with affection when a cat folds itself into this position. It makes them seem vulnerable and innocent. It makes me want to move heaven and earth to keep them safe.

   I tried to help the woman clean up the mess that they had left. There was broken crockery, mud from the herb plant pots and sugar from a broken sugar bowl all over the floor. There was not much I could do to help though, and she was so relieved to have the cats all caught that she thanked me and I took the cats away for neutering. They were only with us a few days until she took the whole family back to live in her garden and kitchen. She was clearly a very caring person.

Rescuing Tails

One of my more memorable rescues took place when I was called out by builders who had started to demolish a shed at an empty council property that was being refurbished. They had found three kittens fast asleep inside the shed, luckily noticing them before having carried out much demolition of the building, although they had made a start.

They were adamant that the shed had to be pulled the rest of the way down that same day and ignored all of our protests that we would need more time than this to get the mother cat so that she could feed her kittens, increasing their chances of survival significantly.

I hurried there, mentally prepared to chain myself to the shed if they tried to knock it down before we the kittens were safe. One of the builders was sympathetic to our cause and sent all the others away on an early and extended lunch. He cheerily let me in but then revealed that they still intended to knock down the shed, and all he could do was to hold the others off for a short while, as long as I promised to deal with the situation as fast as I could.

The problem was, you never know how long a situation like that is going to take.

Celia called me a few times, panicking that they were going to take the shed down with the little ones inside. I did my best to reassure her that I would not let that happen and that I would personally camp in the shed until I had caught the mother cat, if necessary.

The shed roof had already been removed and most of the contents were now in the garden. The builder showed me the kittens, still asleep on an old mattress inside the shed, cosy and undisturbed. There were three tiny kittens, only about one week old, still with their eyes closed. Whilst I was looking through the bedding to check that there were no more kittens, I thought I spotted one, but it was not a kitten, it was half the tail of a fully-grown tortoiseshell cat.

I placed the three babies on a heat pad in a carrier while I searched the rest of the shed for any others.

Celia called me again, asking how I was going to know which cat was the mother as I was not going to have time to do any investigation.

I said, 'Well, I have not seen her yet, but I know that she is a brindle tortoiseshell and I know she is missing half a tail.'

That certainly did not help the already agitated Celia. She said she would come straight down. She was expecting us to find a weak, dying, infected cat. I asked her not to come yet as the builders were already annoyed at my insistence on catching the mother too.

The builder made me a cup of tea (builder strength, though, and almost undrinkable, but it was very kind of him). He let me set up my trap and hide myself inside the patio door. I tried use a dust sheet as a disguise as there were no curtains to stop the cat from seeing me when she arrived. It was two hours before she finally turned up. The builders had managed to find other jobs to do but were insisting that they would have to move onto the shed any minute.

Normally I would think two hours was good for any cat to appear, but in this case, the relief was palpable from everyone. The tail must have healed by itself. There was no indication of any infection. It was just much shorter than it should have been. She actually looked healthy.

I named her Bluebell from the road that we were on — Bluebell Avenue. I was worried that she might find her kittens missing and ignore the food to go in search of them. She did go into the shed and for a few minutes was out of my view, but she reappeared looking unworried. She must not yet have noticed. She headed straight for the food inside the trap.

I trapped her immediately and let out the breath I had been holding, for what felt like the whole of the last two hours, in a huge sigh of relief. But Bluebell was not happy. She went absolutely wild. She tore around the trap desperately trying to get out. I locked it quickly and put a large dark sheet over her. She stopped running but I could hear her still panting heavily in panic. I decided not to put her back in with her kittens just yet, so that she would not associate them with this horrible situation, or accidentally trample them. The builder thanked me gratefully and helped me load them all into my van. He said he would speak to the neighbours to see if anyone knew of Bluebell. He suggested that he might try to raise a donation for Bluebell too, which was very nice of him. He did not manage to find an owner but did deliver a donation, partly collected from the builders themselves.

Back at the clinic, we neutered Bluebell and let her wake up with her babies beside her, so that they would soothe her. Her tail had already healed by itself nicely so nothing further had to be done to it. It was impossible to tell what had caused it to fall off. Bluebell continued to care lovingly for her kittens, but she herself soon proved to be violently feral.

It is very difficult to rehome a feral cat yet but of course, somehow a home must be found. We spent a lot of time trying to find out who, if anyone, had been feeding her to see if they would let us return her to the same place. No feeder could be found, so once her kittens were rehomed, Bluebell was placed with another group of feral cats with whom she fortunately got along well and was eventually rehomed with them to a farm.

Normally the charity would try to keep a mother cat with one of her kittens, because mother cats can suffer when they lose all their babies. But this was a choice of either putting a tame kitten in a feral home, or Bluebell in an indoor home. Neither of these were fair. We had to make the upsetting decision to separate them from her. This led however to the three fortunate kittens all going to one home together.

The Mad Cat Gentleman

I had recently assisted Celia and Naomi with one of the charity newsletters. They had written an article reminding everyone of the importance of befriending and assisting people in vulnerable situations as they were likely to get into trouble again later down the line if they did not trust the charity. The intention was to teach them why we do things the way we do, to encourage them to work with us to help them and their pets. I was supposed to be well-versed on how best to approach these difficult situations.

It was a nice summer morning when I walked into reception to a room full of concerned faces. Everyone was listening to Iris in reception, who turned out to be on the phone to a woman in East Ham with a cat in her garden. She had thrown water on it, thinking that this would make it leave her garden. Instead, it had crawled away from her and collapsed further up the garden. Everyone was absolutely horrified that she could have thrown water on it, whether she had realised that it was ill or not.

I hurried there not really knowing what to expect. I just knew that if the cat that had not run away from water being on it, there must be something very, very wrong with the cat.

When I got there the woman explained that she had not meant to throw water directly on it but when she normally threw water near it, it would run away and leave her garden. But for some reason it had not this time. It had just dragged itself away and collapsed. So she was worried about it.

I picked the cat up, she was completely 'flat' – a term I had heard Celia used to describe extremely weak, floppy cats. She was noticeably dehydrated and had blood all over her tail, with flies buzzing around her. I feared it could be a pyometra — a deadly womb infection.

The vets put her on the operating table immediately, discovering quickly that it was not a pyometra. It was labour gone wrong. The kittens still inside her were already dead. The mother cat was put on antibiotics and a drip immediately. This all happened while I was rushing back to the house in East Ham, shortly followed by my banging on the woman's door, then begging her to let me back through to look for any kittens that may have been born already.

The woman did not think there were any, but I insisted that I must check, so she let me through. She then had an idea of who the cat's owner might be. So while I looked around the garden, she went to find out if she was correct.

Under the compost bin, I found only one kitten, which had very likely never been alive. I put the tiny body in a bag to take it back with me for cremation.

By the time I was satisfied that there were no more, the woman returned to tell me that she had found the owner of the cat. It was a man, whose garden backed onto hers. She gave me his door number, and so I went around to introduce myself and find out what had happened.

I was met by a frantic Asian man, already waiting at the door. He introduced himself as Harry. He had a strong, working-class London accent.

He kept saying, 'Thank you so much for coming' and 'I did not know what to do' while pulling my arm gently, hurrying me through the corridors of his block of flats. I did not really know what he was talking about. I had not told him about his cat, although the neighbour must have told him that we had her. I noticed a sign on the back of the door of his flat as we passed it with a list of daily tasks like 'have a shower'. He caught me noticing it and said his social worker had helped him make it. Then he pulled me through into his bedroom.

Cat Rescuer

I was completely unprepared for this, expecting to be going to explain to him what had happened to his cat. Just as I was about to get annoyed, he let go of me and picked up two tiny kittens from the bed. Still alive, still breathing, only one day old.

They looked warm, cosy, and surprisingly healthy, still sleeping happily in Harry's hands.

He explained that they had been born the night before. Their mother had fed them for a short while, then asked to be let out, as she normally would – he did not have a litter tray. He had let her out, but she had not come back.

He had not known what to do and it had been too dark to go looking for her. He had managed to drip-feed cow's milk to the kittens. They could not survive on this for long, but it seemed to have given them enough strength to keep them alive for the night. I congratulated him for this. He was relieved to let me take the kittens into the clinic to their mother.

She was still much too ill to feed them but was so pleased to see them that we let her give them a wash while Iris got the kitten milk ready. She fed them in reception while doing her work. There is nothing like an animal friendly environment to instil great multi-tasking skills. The customers loved to watch her feed them.

Once these little ones had full tummies, they were put back in with their mother, where they all snuggled up together. It would have been too much of a shame to separate her again from them after such a happy reunion. They stayed with her in the intensive care ward and were hand fed regularly while the mother cat did the rest.

As they grew, it became obvious that one of them had been affected by the difficult birth.

Nichola Kirk

Of the two kittens, one was black and the other was a longhaired tabby, who was nicknamed Forrest. Forrest grew up to be very slow and a bit wobbly. His brother was perfectly normal and bouncy. He ran around like lightning and enjoyed running up and pouncing on Forrest, rolling him to the ground. The nurses would let the two boys out to have a play around the ward, giggling at their antics. While Forrest struggled to stand, his brother would pounce on him and play-bite his neck and push him over. Forrest would try to play back but would always lose. Whenever he did get a grip, his brother would run away and Forrest would jump forward intending to chase him, then tumble immediately over. Forrest loved to play this game but would take a minute to get back on his feet. It was such great natural physiotherapy for Forrest that he did not need any more help than his super playful brother to teach him everything he needed to know. Celia said he probably had Cerebellar hypoplasia. He always stayed a bit on the small side. Nevertheless, he was successfully rehomed at four months old with his brother. This was to a couple who had sadly had their elderly cat pass away. Their cat had had the same disability.

The mother cat eventually recovered too. I took her back, neutered of course, to Harry as he could not drive and we did not want her going on the bus.

I was invited in to let her out in his living room. He had never mentioned that he had more cats. I suppose I should have asked. In the living room, there were cats everywhere. There were two on the sofa, one asleep on the windowsill, a bunch of kittens running about and at one watching me through the open back door.

He asked me to look at one of the cats who was limping. He pointed out the one on the windowsill. It was a huge, male tabby. The cat rolled onto his side as I went over, hoping for a tummy rub. I had a look at his paw and could see he had cut it. I am not a vet of course and was not sure whether it would heal on its own or not. I offered to take him back to the clinic with me for a check-up. He then showed me the mother of the kittens that were running around. He did not want any more kittens but did not know how to stop her from having them. They were about six weeks old and weaning, so would be fine without her for the night. I took her back with me too. I sat and played with the kittens briefly whilst I chatted with Harry to find out as much as possible about his cats. The kittens were beautiful, chubby little things. Harry asked for our help with rehoming them but was happy to keep hold of them until homes were found. He said his other cat was male and that he would get him neutered as soon as he could afford it, now he knew how important it was.

I called him the next day to find out if he could pick his cats up. The foot of the male had been cleaned and the cat would be fine to go home if kept indoors until fully healed. The girl would also need to be kept in for a few days but had to go back to her kittens. He said he did not have the bus fare to get in to pick up the cats and asked if I could take them to him. We were so desperate for the space, and it was only a five-minute drive to East Ham. He had told me that he did not have a litter tray, so I took one with me, and Harry picked up some cat litter ready from his local shop.

I let the two out into his bedroom (there were only two small rooms in the flat) and re-iterated the importance of keeping them indoors for a few days. He promised to be careful when opening the door to let the other two in and out.

It turned out he only managed to keep them in for one day before he decided it was not worth the smell of the litter tray and let them back out again. I did not find this out until much later, but luckily neither cat developed an infection.

Once his other litter were eight weeks old, I repeatedly tried to contact him to arrange to pick them up. When he eventually answered, he said he had not been able to cope with the kittens in his house and had given them to the pet shop. I could not believe it. I contacted the pet shop but they had already sold them.

I had known that he was a vulnerable person and perhaps I should have kept in better contact with him. He had my mobile number, though, and had called me before. I had expected him to keep in touch with me if he had been struggling.

Harry did get his male neutered later with our help again. He moved away a while later, hopefully taking the cats with him, and changed his number. I am sure after such a stressful experience he will be more careful about getting any future cats neutered, but it would have been nice to stay updated.

Windsor The Second

A man walked into the clinic with a kitten in his hands. At the clinic, we have all experienced cats jumping out of people's arms and running into the road, sometimes straight under the wheels of a car, or sometimes just running and running until they are completely lost and are never seen again.

As soon as Iris noticed the kitten, she yelled out, '*cat in arms*!'

I jumped up and ran to the outer door to close it, asking those outside to wait there for a moment. Debbie jumped up and grabbed a cat carrier from the 'for sale' stock in the corner, asking for it to be placed inside. Debbie was the other receptionist of the three. She had short blond hair, possibly dyed, possibly natural. She used to laugh a lot and was incredibly organised, busy and innocent most of the time, then loved to shock us by throwing in the odd rude comment.

This kitten was a tiny, fluffy ginger. Probably only four or five weeks old. The man explained that his friend owned a clothing shop on Balaam Street in East Ham, who found this tiny creature in her shop.

We asked the obvious question: 'how did it get there?'

He did not know. He was called in by his friend, who had a phobia of cats. The kitten had been just sitting in the middle of the room, so he picked him up and brought him straight in to us without really thinking about of there were others.

I asked for the details of the clothing shop, which was in Balaam Street in Plaistow, then took the kitten through to the office. He would have to wait in there until we could find somewhere to house him. It was kitten season again and we had no room, as usual. Si got the kitten out back as soon as I put the carrier down, giving him a cuddle and letting him walk up and down the desk. The kitten was confidently pouncing on the phone wires, pawing at the screens and being utterly cute. Iris mushed him up some kitten food to see if he could eat. He hungrily buried his face in it, leaving his whiskers covered in food. I headed straight out to the shop where he had been found. I wanted to find out; where was its mother? Where were its littermates? How did it get into the shop? Could it have been left there intentionally?

The shopkeeper seemed truly terrified of cats and she was happy let me through, if only to make sure there were no more there.

She pointed out the spot where she had first seen the kitten. It was in the back of the shop, where customers would not have access, in the middle of a corridor with storage rooms leading off it. Clearly it had not been put there by people, as no one would have access. She left me to it while I searched every inch to find the rest of the litter. I could not find any more kittens, nor was there was any obvious way of them getting into the room. There were not even any external doors that could have been left open. I was stumped as to how he could have gotten there.

I went back to the exact spot that the shop owner pointed to and stood staring at my feet at where they said they found him. I crouched down and turned full circle, looking for whatever I had missed, feeling like a detective, but not a very good one so far. I stood back up when I felt a drip hit my head. I looked up to see a hole in the ceiling.

It was difficult to see what might be up there. I borrowed a very unsteady stepladder from the shopkeeper and climbed up to stick my head up through the hole. I could see a cavity space above the building, almost like a loft space, covered in fibreglass insulation. I wondered if the litter and mother cat could be in there and shone the torch. But the insulation rose slightly and then dipped down again and I could not see over the rise.

On the other side, the sloped roof ended, leading outside onto a flat roof.

I eased my way back down the unstable ladder to grab a pouch of kitten food in the hope that there was something nearby to smell it. I threw a couple of pieces onto the flat roof. I tried to be quiet, although every slight movement was making the ladder creak. Within only a minute, an adult cat jumped out of the loft-type space and over onto the flat roof, almost making me leap out of my skin as it jumped almost over my head.

She was a brindle tortoiseshell, so I knew she was definitely female, and also very likely to produce ginger kittens. This must be the mother cat that I was looking for.

I manoeuvred myself on the ladder to lean against the roof to free my hands, freeing my hands to throw some more food towards the cat. The first bit that I threw caused her to run off and almost go over the wall. I froze and she stopped running. She stood watching me while I tried very hard to stay perfectly still despite my uncomfortable, precarious position. I tried not to stare at her as that makes cats nervous.

She watched me for so long that I started to think my toes were going to break from holding my weight in the same position, tiptoeing on the ladder. Eventually, finally, she inched her way back towards me to the food. She sniffed at it, then started to eat hungrily. I moved even slower than before to throw more meat. She backed away again, but not as far as before. I just needed to get her close enough and then work out a way to scruff her from above me and lower her through the small hole, past me without getting my face scratched, down the ladder and into a basket.

I threw some more food towards her and she pounced on it straight away. Once she had almost finished those few bites, I threw some more a little closer to me. She jumped on that too. I started to think perhaps she was a tame cat living stray for a while so had developed some nervousness. I threw more. She moved forward, getting close but watching me very carefully now, poised to run at any sudden movement.

By the time I had used half the pouch, she was not far away. I tipped the rest out in front of me, close enough that I would be able to reach to scruff her. I left my hand resting near the food. She would have to pass my hand to get to the food.

She came close enough for me to touch. I lifted my hand slightly.

She came another step. I brushed my hand gently against her fur.

She came another step. I brushed my hand against her again, leaving it touching her gently.

She was so close. I just needed her to take one more step.

But the touch was too much for her and she turned and ran over the wall and out of sight.

I knew she would not come back anytime soon. I did not dare leave any more food up there because of the risk that the other kittens up there somewhere could fall down the hole, like their sibling must have. It was approximately a seven-foot drop but there was nothing I could do to block it as I would need help — if only someone to hold the ladder steady.

I needed to figure out where she was keeping the rest of the kittens.

I informed the shopkeeper of what had happened and told her that I would be returning the following day with help. Back at the clinic Si had gone for the day, so the kitten was back in his carrier, along with his now empty food bowl and snuggled up cosily in a blanket.

There is a common saying that, 'Cats always land on their feet'. And while this is true, it does not mean that they do not frequently break their legs in the process of falling from high places and landing on their feet. It was amazing that such a small little thing had not been at all harmed by such a big fall.

We could not find anywhere in the clinic for him to go. There was not a cage, or even a cat-free space in the building, and he could not be left on his own with older cats. He was much too small to look after himself. There was not even a foster cat with kittens his age that could take him on temporarily. He ended up coming back to my room with me. I was sleeping in one room at the clinic at the time and so would have to keep him in my bedroom. Being mildly allergic to cats, I tried to not have them in my bedroom if it could be avoided. But the little ginger kitten was so sweet and there was nowhere else for him to comfortably go. Celia already had cats in her bedroom too (and in every room of her flat), and everyone else had their own cats so could not foster easily.

I nicknamed him Windsor II, partly because he looked just like another kitten that I had fostered a while before from Windsor Terrace (I was hardly going to name this one 'Balaam'). I only expected to have him for a couple of days until I had caught his family and could arrange a foster home to care for them all together. He was so hyper and playful. He used my hand as a toy, biting it and kicking it for an hour, before eating, then falling asleep back in his carrier.

By the next morning, I had lots of itchy, swollen lines across my hand where he had scratched my skin. I had not noticed his tiny claws scratching me while we played. I washed myself thoroughly, took an antihistamine and tried to ignore it.

Windsor II slept in his carrier next to my bed, with a miniature litter tray made out of a takeaway dish, and his water and food nearby. I fell in love with him, of course. I did with all of those that came home with me. It was difficult knowing I would have to give him up at some point.

Cat Rescuer

I always tried to distance myself and not get involved emotionally, but it never did work.

While he was all snug and cosy in my room, I spent the day out looking for his family, hoping to reunite them all very soon.

I took Si with me to help me set up his movement-triggered night-vision camera. He tied it up on an upright post holding up the roof, positioned to look down into the loft space, as this is where I had assumed the kittens would be. He also helped me set up a makeshift, miniature version of a dummy trap in the space. It was too small for a normal trap. Then he used some thick plastic sheeting to lay across the rest of the hole, so no curious kittens could fall.

Si had picked up the camera and uploaded the images to the computer before I had even woken up the next morning. As I worked into the evening, the clinic was only without a rescue worker for maybe four hours a night. Even then, either Celia, Pete, Angie or I were asleep nearby, and willing to get up in case of an emergency that could not wait until Si got there.

The camera had taken over a hundred photos in just the one night. We went over them many times, looking at every detail. There was a ginger cat, a black longhaired cat, and the brindle mother cat. She caught a rat and it was fascinating to see it happen in the freeze-framed images. She carried it off out of sight of the camera. There was no sign of any kittens and it did not look like the mother was spending much time there either. So if they were not in the loft space, where were they?

I went to put food inside the dummy trap the next day and asked Pete to keep this up over the weekend. Windsor II came home with me, teasing my neighbour's cat by pawing at the conservatory window and sleeping lots on my then fiancé's lap while he played on the computer. All weekend, I worried about where his family were. I even had dreams about climbing up through the hole and crawling about, exploring further. But in real life I would not have fitted through.

On Monday, I returned with a determination to search continually until I found them. I went into many of the neighbouring properties that overlooked the flat roof but could not see any sign of where they might be.

I went back to the clinic to Google the area, using the maps to get a better idea of what was surrounding the shop. As a result of this, I went to the Job Centre a few doors down. It was a huge building, and might give me a better vantage point.

The Job Centre were initially unsure about my request to look out of their windows. But a security guard had an idea. He took me up many flights of stairs, and at least three floors of offices. I was amazed by how many people work at the job centre behind the scenes. All were curious about my little adventure and the cat carrier in my hands.

The security guard took me out of a fire-exit onto a flat roof, but at the wrong side of the building.

We had to walk on the roof along a narrow front of the building (it probably was not particularly narrow, but I am not great with heights), then climb a vertical steel ladder to an even higher part of the building. I had to leave the carrier behind to climb, but took my bag of food pouches with me.

At the end of the highest roof was another vertical ladder going back down the other side. It felt too high and steep for me. But I made it down. We looked down over the neighbouring shops. From this angle, I could see what surrounded the shop's flat roof but there was no way to get down onto it.

Cat Rescuer

I saw that the chicken shop next door to the clothing shop had a back yard, which might be a good area to look. I could also see an alleyway running along the backs of all the shops, with a gate for access. I had not realised this was there before because the clothing shop did not have any access to the alley.

I went to investigate. I checked every nook and cranny in the alley to be sure no kittens were there. At the end of the alley, some men were chatting out the back of a shop taking a break. They did not speak very good English but understood enough to tell me that they saw the tortoiseshell cat frequently, and looked after their own cat there too, a ginger boy. They had not seen any kittens.

I considered climbing up the end building, using the corner of the wall, to see if it was possible to get onto the roof of the clothing shop. To get a better look at how the buildings connected I first climbed onto some piled up pallets. But the buildings were not connected closely enough. I was about to climb down when I saw a movement in the corner of my eye. I had not quite pinpointed where it had been so stood on my tiptoes on the pallets, watching.

A tortoiseshell kitten soon came bounding out into view. It was frolicking along a drainpipe that ran along the side of the clothing shop, within the chicken shop's yard. The kitten ran back along the drainpipe, then disappeared out of view into a hole created by an edge between two roofs. Moments later, she came rolling back out, play-fighting with another kitten.

I wanted to jump up and down in excitement, but I was balanced far too precariously for that. Instead, I stood with a huge grin on my face, watching them play.

There were three kittens: the tortoiseshell, a ginger and a black and white.

The drainpipe was overhanging the yard of the chicken shop, which had a locked gate into the alley.

I walked back around the front and begged the chicken shop for access to the back. They could not let me through without the boss' permission. They said I would need to come back when he was there the next day at midday.

The next day I returned to the chicken shop as agreed. They informed me that the manager would not now be in that day and so they still could not let me through. I asked to them to ask for his permission. Immediately.

They called him, but then passed the phone to me so I could explain. Then he told them to let me through. They took me through the kitchen and out the back door into a small yard. I found the spot where the kittens were and thankfully, they were out and playing on the drainpipe, so I could point them out to the shop worker, proving my reason for being there.

The drainpipe was about nine feet high, completely out of reach. Just underneath it was the sloped roof of an outhouse that was right next to the kittens' hiding place. I put some food on top of the outhouse roof, to see if the kittens could get down to it. I knew that even if I could get up to them, they would just hide in their hole so there was no chance of me grabbing them. And there was nowhere that the trap could be balanced safely at that height.

The kittens could barely get anywhere at all. They could not even get down onto the lower roof. They were stuck with only their hole, and the length of the drainpipe to play on.

I had no idea how to get them down, so that evening, I described the scene to Celia to ask for her expert advice and she suggested a 'kitten ladder'. I had never used one of these before so she explained how. It was simply a long length of wood, with blocks of wood tied to it at intervals that the kittens could more easily step onto.

We had intended to get the handyman to make one for us, but he was not going to be available for a few days. While I was there feeding them the next day, I decided to have a go at improvising a kitten ladder. I borrowed a long length of wood from the shop at the end. I tied some small lengths of wood across the very long piece to make steps. Despite its length, the ladder still made quite a steep slope for such little kittens to use and I still needed a way to help the kittens get down onto the lower roof.

I borrowed Pete and a stepladder from the clinic. He held the ladder while I climbed up and tied a couple of milk-crates onto the lower roof of the outhouse, giving the kittens a step down.

We waited to see if the kittens could use the steps, but they did not appear. I suspected it was because we had made so much noise setting everything up so near to their hiding place. I left the ladder in place so that they could get used to it overnight.

The next day, one of the chicken-shop staff met me excitedly and hurried me through, pointing down at a sheltered area, underneath an old chest freezer that was stored in the yard, saying, 'kittens'.

I grabbed my trap as quickly as I could and set it up at the bottom of the ladder and backed off as far as I could go in the tiny yard.

Shortly after, two kittens came running out from under the freezer, playing, rolling each other over and bounding around happily. They were curious about the food, although they only ate a few bites. Fortunately, they soon decided that the trap was a great toy too, and both ended up inside at the same time. I caught them quickly and transferred them into a carrier in the van.

Then I set back up to catch the last black and white kitten, and with any luck, the mother.

Whilst I was waiting, I met the little ginger cat that belonged to the neighbours. He was a perfectly normal ginger cat in most ways. But the odd thing about him was that he had red eyes. When I mentioned him that evening, Celia said there was a possibility of the red eyes being caused by Corona virus. I tried to explain this to his owners to see if they wanted him tested. They did not want this but did at least get him neutered. There was no more I could do about the virus except hope it never mutated to FIP. Many cats unsuspectingly have Corona virus as it does no harm to them. It can turn into the nasty Feline Infectious Peritonitis, which causes fatal fluid build-up, particularly in the lungs.

I continued to go every day, but was struggling to catch the last kitten. It came out each day and played on the drainpipe but showed no interest whatsoever in coming down the ladder. He ignored my trail of treats completely, no matter what I used, and insisted on chasing his own tail instead.

His brother and sister were rehomed together straight away. Windsor II stayed with me. At 11pm each night, the chicken shop staff came out and told me that I would have to leave as they needed to lock the back gate. One night, the kitten had come down further than ever before. I was not going to be able to come back for a few days, so I begged to stay a little longer. They gave me twenty minutes, but the kitten still did not come down the rest of the way.

I gave them strict instructions of where to feed and when to feed and what to do if the kitten came down and gave them telephone numbers enough to cover the few days that I would not be there.

Cat Rescuer

I briefed Celia and Pete on what was going to happen with the Chicken Shop job over the weekend, and tried to put their minds at rest that the mother and kitten would be fed, and that they would be in a good routine by the time I got back, ready to be caught.

Windsor II stayed at the clinic for the weekend as I could not take him with me to my parents, who had dogs. When I got back on the Monday, they had already found him a home. I was very upset to not have been able to say goodbye but pleased but pleased he had a permanent family to love him. He went to live with a family with a young boy and another kitten, who had gotten lonely by himself and needed some company. I had thought we would keep hold of him until we caught his brother from the guttering, but this was better than keeping him at the clinic any longer. He would be happy with the attention he would get from the boy and the other kitten.

I spent the first few days that week making further adjustments to my kitten ladder and trying to coax Windsor II's brother down the ladder. His mother started to appear frequently and used the ladder happily. Each day the black and white would come down a little further.

On the Thursday I was called to an emergency instead where some kittens had been found living in wasteland beside a pub. One had been picked up by someone coming out of the pub and taken with them. I tried to find out who that had been so I could ensure it had gone to a safe secure home. All my enquiries led to dead ends. The kittens had grown up wild and so I doubted if anyone had really managed to get hold of one. But it certainly was not worth the risk leaving them there, especially as just around the corner was a busy high street.

It took me a few days to catch them. The day after I caught them, I was setting up the van ready to get back to the chicken shop. That moment, the shop's manager called me to let me know that the kitten had come down the ladder overnight. He had amazingly managed to catch him in his own carrier. He was on his way to bring him into us for a check-up and wanted to keep him after.

At his check-up however, the nurses discovered that somehow the kitten had burnt his paws.

No one knew how it had happened. He had also managed to singe his whiskers. We could only theorise that he must have somehow either ended up jumping on the barbeque next door, if it had been left uncovered with some hot coals still on it or have gotten into the chicken shop and onto their grill. He had been in the yard when they found him. We suspected that this was the reason why he had been so easy for them to pick up, despite having never been touched by humans before.

He was in intensive care for a while. He had huge bandages wrapped around his feet for a couple of days, but he healed quickly. He was always a little nervous, so the manager's family agreed to adopt a different, friendlier kitten. They came in to give the black and white kitten a fuss but, in the end, we recommended that his children needed a more confident cat to cuddle and play with. The black and white kitten was rehomed with a male tabby with whom he had made friends while recovering.

I went back and caught his mother easily in the trap. She was scarily feral. It was incredible that she had ever let me get close enough to touch her. The chicken shop agreed to have her back and take her on officially. They made her a bed in a sheltered area in their yard and bought her the best food.

Windsor II soon after had to come back into the clinic. He had horrible diarrhoea and got quite dehydrated and ill with it. He had been put on a special diet and various medication with which his new owners could not keep up. So I got to look after him for the weekend at my own home. He had a great time bullying the neighbour's cat by puffing his fur out and jumping sideways aggressively when she came past the patio door. I think he was trying to look aggressive, but he was so tiny and cute that it made me laugh every time he did it. He watched some films with us and chewed on our hands and pounced on his feather toy. The next week, he was back to normal and could go home. I made sure I was there this time to hand him back over to his owner. The little boy clearly already loved him and his dad was very sweet and seemed to have been worrying a lot about him. I enjoyed meeting them, it made me feel so much better seeing for myself how lovely the family was. I loved fostering, despite the hard work, but the hardest part was most definitely giving them up at the end.

A Mad Cat Lady

This is one of the most frightening yet exhilarating jobs that I ever completed during my time as an animal rescue officer.

The story started with one mother cat with kittens eating with some other strays in Stepney. The kittens had been born in a summerhouse and the feeders had only realised the kittens were there since they had been big enough to start coming out to the food. We picked up, tamed and rehomed the kittens, and neutered and returned the adults.

Whilst Si was returning the final male, he was approached by a woman who told him that they were all her cats and she was very unhappy that they had been neutered. She asked him not to touch any more of her cats. He of course explained that they had been assumed stray as they were very nervous and had given birth outside. He advised that if not neutered, and particularly whilst pregnant, she should keep her cats indoors to prevent the same situation occurring again, as people would certainly worry about them and expect them to be strays. She accepted this and agreed to do so. She was aggressively against neutering. As Si had neutered all the ones fed by the first lady to report the situation, we decided not to get further involved. There were many other cats that we could help without needing to get involved with hostile people. So we left it at that.

A few months later we received a call from a social worker asking us to attend a property in Stepney where a woman named Francine had not been seen for several weeks. There was a suggestion that the lady could have passed away but her cats were still at the property.

We attended, prepared for the worst, with lots of food, and lots of carriers. Si pointed out the house where he had neutered cats and reminded me of the woman who had not wanted her cats neutered. But he had not known where she lived. At this point we had no reason to suspect that the two stories were linked.

The police turned up, along with the social workers. They made several attempts to draw the attention of anyone at the house, knocking on the door and windows and yelling through the letterbox. They had posted letters days before and no one had responded.

Once they had determined that no one was home, or at least unable to answer the door, they called a locksmith, who took a while trying to get the door open, and soon resorted to drilling the lock out, making an awful lot of noise.

He pushed the door open to reveal a surprising scene. Full bin bags and random items, like a carpet, duvets, mismatched chairs and mess filled the corridor, the stairs, and as far as we could see, as high as my waist. Cats were everywhere, on every surface. A woman was walking very slowly down the stairs in her nightgown (this was early afternoon), navigating her way through the chaos. This, we presumed, was the missing person, Francine. She was clearly very much still alive.

The social workers had a long chat with her about why she had not responded to them and discussed how they could help her to look after herself better.

After this, we were introduced to her. Si recognised her as the woman who had approached him when he dropped off the neutered cats and she recognised him too. We explained that the many kittens visible that were snotty and sneezing were clearly suffering from cat flu. She seemed to understand and to trust Si and know of Celia and respect her. Many of the kittens had at least one infected eye. One particular little one's eyes were so infected that they were glued shut and it was walking around effectively blind.

Whilst Si discussed future plans to help her get the kittens treated for flu, I got out some cotton wool and a bottle of water and cleaned the eyes of all the kittens I could get my hands on, paying extra special attention to the little one with two bad eyes. I was relieved to find it still could see once its eyes were opened. It looked rather dazed and confused, as though being able to see was a new and frightening experience for it.

We explained that once we had treated the cat flu, it would be best if she would allow us to neuter some of her cats to manage the number, as there must have already been over twenty cats crammed into this small maisonette, and overcrowding would just lead to recurring cat flu. She seemed happy with this and gave us her number to arrange an appointment to return with a vet and flu medications. We left on good terms.

Over the next few months, I called and left multiple voicemails, knocked on her door and posted notes through her door (until she had her letterbox sealed up). We tried to get help again from the social worker, but she did not have any luck contacting her either.

It was heart breaking to think of those poor kittens and there was nothing we could do.

About a year later, the following January, we had a call to the same area about some kittens that were living under a bush beside a wall. At the time I had not made the link, but I soon found out that it was likely to be the same house.

We were told that they appeared to have flu and did not seem to have any accessible shelter despite the cold, wet weather. The caller was experienced with cats and had been feeding them since they had appeared. The kittens were too nervous for her to get hold of. She had recently seen one get killed by a passing dog and was very upset that these were still so exposed. Although the dog's owner had felt terrible and agreed to keep his dog on its lead in future, she was still worried that it, or another dog, could still get to them.

They would have been totally exposed had the caller not provided them with a large piece of wood propped against the wall under the bush. The feeder said she had argued with the 'owner' accusing her of interfering since putting the wood there. But they were too small to get up the wall and there was nowhere else to hide. The kittens had not even been born in the 'owner's house. The feeder told us that they had been born in one of the sheds in the row of houses on the other side of the wall.

The area behind the house was a large green square, with pathways criss-crossing it and surrounded by maisonette style council flats. I still had Francine's number in my phone so I tried to call her, but of course, there was no answer. I posted her a folded note by her front door explaining that I was there and asking if any of the cats from the patch of grass behind her property were hers. The wall was at least six feet high, I could not see over it even if I jumped. There was thick ivy growing over it from Francine's garden at the end, but the wall ran continuously, enclosing about eight gardens to one side of her.

The shed that kittens had been born in had a hole in the roof, which was just visible above the wall, three gardens along.

I waited under a tree with a notepad to avoid sitting in the snow and made a note of all the cats I saw. The caller brought kindly brought out a cup of tea to help me keep warm. I put food down beside me on a paper plate to test which of the cats were willing to come close to me, and how easy they would be to catch — if it came to it. They were almost all suffering with flu. There seemed to be two litters;

a black mother with four black kittens, and a tabby mother with three smaller kittens. There was 'black with white whiskers' and 'white with black whiskers' and 'half moustache' and 'fluffy boy', and many others. These became my names for them. Even Celia ended up memorising these odd nicknames without ever having seen them. 'What's happening with Fluffy boy?' she would ask.

One male tabby was so friendly that he snuggled on my lap the whole evening, occasionally rolling over or patting my hand with a paw for more attention. He was the only one that seemed to like attention. The black kittens were tame enough that they would eat right next to me, but not so much that they would let me touch them without flinching. The three smaller kittens would not come anywhere near me. Nor would the two mothers. A pregnant tabby was so nervous that she stayed up on the wall the whole time I was there and would not even come down further along the wall for food. It was unusual to find kittens and pregnant cats at this time of year. But although it was cold and frosty, warm weather had continued late into the winter, allowing more cats to come into season much later in the year than they normally would. This was putting a huge amount of extra pressure on the charity.

The next day, after discussing with Celia the best course of action, we decided that we had to act as it was far too dangerous to leave the kittens where they were, due both to their flu and due to their exposure to threats. If Francine were to approach me and declare that she owned the kittens, she would be legally responsible for cruelty for not having taken proper care of them and sought veterinary treatment, as well as not providing food, shelter or socialisation. I attended that day with the intention of trying to catch the ill kittens and any pregnant cats, so that they would not also have to give birth outside in the cold, and for their kittens to suffer the same unhappy life.

Cat Rescuer

Soon after I arrived however, Francine opened her rear upstairs window yelling, 'Oi, what are you doing with my cats?!'

I waved and called back, 'Hi Francine, remember me? I'm from cat rescue. Do you know anything about these ill kittens down here?'

She could not hear me properly, so I asked her to come out to me. As she approached, marching aggressively towards me, in a dressing gown, she again yelled, 'What are you doing with my cats?'

I re-introduced myself. She claimed she had not received any of my notes, calls or messages. I double checked her phone number and she confirmed it was correct. I explained what I was doing and why I was feeding the cats. I explained that I had to take in the ill kittens for treatment. She denied ownership of the kittens, and of any pregnant cats. She was clearly aware that she would be in trouble if she claimed to own them. She agreed that they must be taken in for treatment, taming and homing.

She pointed out two cats that were 'hers'. The very healthy, friendly tabby boy, who was sitting nearby, whom she called Peter, and a black cat sat on the wall, longhaired with a dot of white on the chin, whom she called Susie.

She said that a black cat of hers had gone missing recently and insisted on checking the back of my van. She was convinced that I had already taken some of her cats, although she would not admit ownership to any other than those two. I willingly showed her the empty van to gain some trust.

She calmed down after this and was talking normally to me, telling me about how she loved her cats and about the interfering neighbour' and her issues with the council trying to evict her, even though she had lived in the house for many years, since when her mother was alive. I almost felt sorry for her until I reminded myself that she had very likely allowed kittens to die of flu and done nothing to save them.

I mentioned that I was quite convinced that Susie was the mother of the black kittens with flu. She did not respond to this and changed the subject. Then she circled round again to say that she did not want me taking her cats. I repeated that I did not intend to take her cats, if I knew which they were and so she must be certain to tell me which hers. I explained why we think it is irresponsible to allow pregnant cats outside, perfectly evidenced by the litters of now feral kittens that had been born in her neighbours' shed, with dreadful, potentially lethal flu. I advised her again that I would be catching any pregnant females I found outside, and that if she did have any that she was not telling me about, that she must keep them indoors from now on for the duration of their pregnancies to ensure that the kittens were born in a safe place. As we talked, a large black tom cat passed us with a very bad limp. She explained that he was a stray who came to harass her cats frequently. She was insistent that he must be caught to be taken in for treatment.

Over the next two weeks, I managed to catch most of the kittens and a few pregnant cats, mostly by hand, but some using a manual trap positioned just a few feet away from me. Clearly most had had some contact with people and had not become completely feral. I had however been unable to catch the tabby mother cat or the black limping male as neither would come anywhere near me, or even the food, no matter how far I put it away from me. I had also decided not to catch Susie, despite being convinced that she was an unneutered female as I did not want to risk breaching Francine's trust whilst I still needed access to the other cats. Those now at the clinic were mostly taming up quickly and gradually getting over their flu. They had to be quarantined

Cat Rescuer

so as not to infect the other cats in the clinic and so were getting lots of attention in the staff room.

Each night, the lovely tabby, Peter, would still come and sit on my lap and we would keep each other warm.

I tried going at different times of day. But at any other time, there was not a cat in sight. They clearly knew their feeding routine too well. So I continued going after six in the evening.

After a couple of weeks, I caught the tabby mother, by putting the trap as far away from me as it would go and hiding behind the ivy. She was put back in with her kittens, even though they were old enough to be rehomed, to help them all feel safe.

I went back night after night, desperate to catch the poor limping male. He never seemed hungry, and always walked by, ignoring me, the food and all the other cats. He left the square through the car park. None of the other cats ventured that far. I assumed he must have another feeder. But when I tried to follow him, he led me in circles, literally. Either he noticed me following him or he was checking on his territory.

One night it was particularly cold and I did not feel like sitting, freezing, under the tree or behind the wall. I tried something different, setting up the trap within reach of the van. After all, the limping cat would usually pass through the car park so it was worth a try, and I would be less visible too, hopefully. Three hours later, he had not turned up at all.

Just when I was about to give up for the night, Francine came out of her house. She was striding towards me angrily and yelling, 'Oi, what are you doing with my cats?'

Her wavy grey hair was flying about in the wind while she threw her arms around erratically. She was wearing a dressing gown and slipper boots. I half-expected her to throw a cat at me, like the cat lady from the Simpsons.

I admit was quite nervous of her that point. Even though I have had some self-defence training, it had been a long time ago and I did not like to use it.

I yelled back 'Hi' in the friendliest voice I could fake. As she got closer, still yelling, I responded again in my most innocent voice, 'Hi, how are you doing?' By the time she got to me, she could not keep up the aggression against my friendliness, thankfully. She visibly slumped in resignation as she asked me again, much more calmly, what I was doing with her cats.

Her yelling and flailing had drawn attention from people in the flats overlooking the car park. I noticed faces peering out from behind many curtains.

I felt rather sorry for Francine. I suspected that all the cats could be hers. I reminded her of what we had previously discussed and explained that I was hoping to catch the limping cat. She told me that he was better now. Despite the cold, we had a long discussion about various leg injuries that cats might get, with my trying to impress the necessity of treatment in many cases, and her describing the miraculous ability of cats to get on with life even when injured and to recover quickly. I made it clear to her that I still intended to check him over.

I was getting colder and colder, shivering, perhaps a little from the receding adrenaline too that had kicked in as she had first approached. I kept trying to end the conversation, so that we could both get back to the warmth. Just as I was thinking this, I looked down to notice the limping cat very close by and heading towards the trap. Francine spotted him too and said, 'See, he's not limping anymore'. She was right.

I said again that I would still be taking him in for a check-up. She became very upset and said that she did not agree with neutering and that we must not take him in because she did not want us to do that to him. He was in the trap, for the first time, and I was going to have to leave him or cause an argument. I agreed not to take him in yet as I could not afford to upset her. There were still more cats here that I wanted to have neutered, in time, and wanted her on our side. I had found that generally if you help someone, they soon come to realise that their cats are much happier once neutered. They become advocates of neutering.

There was also the thought that once a cat has eaten in a trap once safely, they will be much more likely to go in again. I let him eat in the trap and kept the lady talking until he had finished and moved on, feeling safe.

I explained the virtues of neutering again and tried to sway her to allow me to neuter Peter and Susie. She was stubbornly against it still.

I was too cold to stay longer. I made excuses to leave and started packing up all my equipment. Francine followed me around the back of my van whilst I packed away, peering in, clearly checking that I did not have any cats. What would she have done if I had? I reminded her that she would have to take responsibility if she allowed her pets to breed. She must assume full ownership and responsibility for any kittens born, rather than leaving them out in the cold to fend for themselves. She accepted all this, nodding along and agreeing with everything I said and saying, 'Of course'. I cautioned her that if I heard that a pregnant cat was out here that I would assume that it was not hers, because she was going to be responsible from now on and keep hers indoors.

She agreed that she would.

I got back to the clinic and sat down with Celia. She offered to buy takeaway for the evening staff as a thank you for our hard work.

While we ate, I explained to Celia that although the limping cat was no longer limping, there were still females in the area. We arranged for Celia to call Francine, to use her skills discussing at length the benefits of neutering as we both felt that she would be able to explain much better than I would why it is so important. I called her there and then. As usual, there was no answer. I left Francine a voicemail, not expecting her to respond. Then I discussed with Celia where all the cats going to be put that had been dumped that day. There had been seven left on the doorstep all in one day.

I went back behind Francine's the next night and caught the black male cat. The only cats now left were either very likely to be male and difficult to catch, and Susie and Peter. After this, I decided not to push my luck with Francine any further and asked the sympathetic neighbours to keep a close eye on the cats for me.

Only a couple of weeks later, the charity received another call from Francine's social worker. She explained that Francine was going to be evicted. It was shortly after the new bedroom tax policy, where people were being moved into council accommodation more relevant to the size of their family, or else taxed for the extra room. Francine lived on her own in a three-bedroom place so they were moving her to a one bedroom flat. They had tried to evict her multiple times before and she had always managed to stop it. But this time, they were determined, and she had been issued with an eviction notice. The council had found a new place to live that suited her better (according to the government rules at least).

We arranged attend a meeting with the council and Francine, to work out an action plan on how to get the cats moved safely to her new place with minimum stress and disruption for everyone. Celia was supposed to be coming with me, but there was a last-minute crisis that she had to deal with. I took Si instead as he was good at tricky negotiations with difficult people. Mostly because he explained the facts in straight, honest terms that showed how their actions would directly impact their own lives. For example, he once convinced a restaurant to have their feral cats back on their land because they were keeping the rats away, and therefore an asset to their business, saving them a fortune in pest control compared to the small cost of cat food and shelters.

Francine did not turn up to the meeting. We used the time with the council to plan for the day to make it as stress-free as possible for Francine, even though she was now accusing us of having stolen her cats. We negotiated how many cats she would be allowed to take with her as we wanted her to be able to keep a few as they would be happier staying together. We advised the council that the woman would be much better-off with a few of her cats (which they insisted were neutered and microchipped). It would probably stop her from thinking of buying or finding a kitten to breed in her new place. The council had initially wanted her to have just one, or none. We managed to convince them to let her have two or three.

In the run up to eviction day, Si, Celia and I made sure our diaries were free. I convinced the other clinic's to take some of our cats so that we would have room.

There were still an incredible thirty-four cats to pick up from outside, and we expected as many again inside. But we had never been so prepared.

I attended with Simon on the first day, both of us with vans full of baskets, and a couple of the staff from the Lewisham clinic. We had been asked to wait away from the property, out of sight, until Francine had been removed from the property. The police were there, and the council had provided removal vans. Francine was supposed to have already chosen and marked the items that she would be taking with her.

Nothing seemed to happen for a while. Everyone was sort of hanging around, waiting. The police then received a call telling them not to enter because Francine had turned up at court for a last-minute hearing to protest her eviction.

While the social worker was trying to find out what to do next, we waited around the back of the property, keeping out the way, while I familiarised my colleagues with the cats. There were not usually many cats at that time of day, but over the course of a couple of hours, all of them seemed to appear briefly.

As we watched, a tabby cat that I did not recognise appeared up on the wall. Closely followed by a little tabby kitten, maybe only six weeks old, then a black and white, and then a black longhaired kitten.

This was the first time I had ever seen them and it made me wonder if she had locked all of her cats outside today in the hope that they would be harder for us to catch.

We had to make the decision of whether to risk trying to catch the kittens and their mother now, without the permission of the owner.

Peter, the tabby, had been there of course. He had been saying hello to everyone, getting lots of fuss and cuddles and purring away until something distracted him. He ran off around the corner.

We decided to try to catch the mother cat and her three kittens. The kittens were much too young to be safe outside on their own, particularly on such a high wall.

Whilst we were trying to make friends with the kittens and mother cat, a black cat came bolting out from where Peter had gone earlier, as if running for her life. She was chased by one of the black and white young cats, then Peter, then the large black cat, then two more black and white cats.

Soon there were nine of them, all chasing the one. Si explained that the cat at the front must be in season, and the rest must be males.

The female eventually ran up into a tree, breathless and wide-eyed. The other cats kept jumping up to try to get to her. When they got too close, she would make an agitated screaming noise at them and whack at them until they fell back down.

They all were trying to mate with her. And she was doing everything she could to avoid it. But without our help, she was not going to manage it. Surely cats deserve protection from something that in humans would be perceived as one the most serious of crimes?

We tried to approach the cat, but she made it very clear that she was too stressed to tolerate us. We set up a trap in the hope that if we could not catch her, she might at least get used to the trap for when we would have to catch her, hoping that we could at least take her away from her tormenters. She did want to eat, but every time she got near the trap, the males would rush her again and she would retreat up the tree.

When it was getting dark, we were finally updated that the woman would still be getting evicted, but it had now been delayed for two weeks. Francine was on her way home. It was heart-breaking but we had to leave the poor female cat behind for the night, as well as the mother and kittens.

We arranged for the cats to be fed during the day instead of feeding at night by a neighbour, so that by the time eviction day came, we would have more time to catch them.

Si went back to the property the next morning, early in the morning, intending to try to catch the female and the little family as Celia could not bear the thought of leaving them unprotected. By the time I arrived, he already had the in-season-female, although he had had to catch some of the males first to get them out of her way. Si had not managed to catch the kittens but they were still on the safe side of the wall. I took over from Si, sharing ideas for catching the rest.

We debated the possibility of raising the trap up onto the wall, but it would be too unstable and might fall when the trap was closed. We thought about making a ladder to help the kittens get down. But then worried that if they got down, and we did not catch them, they would be stuck.

Si went the next morning and managed to hand-grab the kittens from the wall, then use them as 'bait' to catch the mother. He returned them to the clinic, then went back to be sure that we had not left any behind.

I called him when I got in to congratulate him and get an update. He did not pick up.

Moments later, I got a picture text of an iron exercise bar saying, 'Francine just tried to hit me with an iron bar!' I called him again and he answered on the first ring. He had been adding fresh food to the traps, when he heard something rummaging around in the back of the van. He had approached slowly, expecting to find a cat looking for food. He stepped around the van and Francine was there looking through his van. As she spotted him, she turned, swinging the heavy bar directly at his head. He had managed to dodge it, but she immediately swung it again. He managed to grab hold of the bar before it hit him, but she would not let go and he had to wrestle it from her. Once she was unarmed, she turned and ran. If it had been me there instead of him, I might not have reacted quickly enough and would have been at least hospitalised, if not killed.

He called the police to report the attempted assault. They tried to find her but had not been able to. She had not gone home. Si was so angry that he decided that he no longer cared about her feelings as to whether the cats were hers or

Cat Rescuer

not. And in one weeks' time, she would only own two of them anyway, if she was not in prison for assault. So he started catching them.

I had to refuse to go there again. I did not feel confident that I could protect myself against an attack with a weapon. It was too much of a risk. Si did not mind, he was doing a great job by himself, as always, and had managed to catch almost all the cats within a week.

Then it was eviction day again. We attended to check the furniture coming out for hidden cats and kittens. It was just me and Si this time, because we were confident that we already had most of the cats back at the clinic.

The police broke into the property, carefully, conscious that they must not allow any cats out, if there were any in there.

As they opened the door, we saw what can only be described as 'rubbish' piled up in the hallway, pressing against the door, making it very difficult for the police to force it open. The last time we had been inside, the year before, there had been a lot of mess and rubbish up to about waist height, with gaps for the door and little pathways through. This time however, the mess was almost touching the ceiling. It was difficult to imagine how Francine even got around the house. We realised then that she was an extreme hoarder and must have serious mental health issues to go with it. Hoarders tend to collect animals, often cats, as well as what the rest of us perceive as rubbish. We explained this to the council and that we recommended that Francine should be referred to a mental health professional.

The police could not check two of the bedrooms because the rubbish was piled so high that they could not physically get to them.

Nichola Kirk

The living room was most impressive. The rubbish was literally touching the ceiling in places. It seemed to consist of chairs, full bin bags, empty plastic bottles and newspapers.

Francine's social worker told us that she had just managed to get in touch with her daughter. I had not previously known she had a daughter, or any family at all. The social worker discovered that Francine was at her daughter's house. They explained that if she did not attend the property to tell them what she wanted to keep, then they would make the decisions on her behalf.

The council removal men put on gloves to clear the hallway. Then they made a start on the landing so that the police could get into the remaining rooms to check them. Then they let us in to check for any cats hiding. In the mess, it was impossible to know whether there were any for certain. We did our best, including checking that all the routes out of the building were closed. At the other end of the living room, we could see a window, and knew there must be a door to the garden, but the mess was piled high, and pressed tightly against the living room door, with only a small space at the very top.

Si turned to me with a cheeky sideways smile, saying 'looks like a job for a small person'. He gave me a leg up into the small space at the top of the rubbish in the living room. There was so much stuff, all tightly compacted together. I had to crawl because, even on my hands and knees, my head was touching the ceiling. I moved slowly; not quite sure how stable the whole thing was likely to be. I inched my way around lots of cat excrement, little piles of cat biscuit, and random objects sticking up through everything else. The smell of the excrement had me trying not to breathe too deeply. The most obvious theme seemed to be piles of mismatched chairs. I managed to get across the room to the back door, completely out of sight by now of the hallway. There was enough room there to get down to the door, with a table to step down on to and a cardboard box with remnants of cat biscuits beside it. The door was closed and locked.

I checked that there were no other exits for the cats. Then I climbed out and gave permission for the removal men to start clearing the room. They had already filled a huge van with the empty flattened cardboard boxes, plastic bottles and other rubbish, taken it to the tip and come back with two vans.

The social worker had managed to convince Francine to come to the property and claim whatever she wished to keep. She was told that if she tried to cross the threshold of the property, she would be trespassing and would be removed by force. We were asked to back off but insisted on being able to watch the door for escaping cats, just in case. The social worker said she could have one van for rubbish and one for things she wanted to keep. She started picking out the most random of things. She was pulling out broken hair curlers and bits of newspaper and box that were already loaded onto the 'rubbish' van and putting them onto the 'keep' van. The social worker later told us that had they have known before of the extremity of her hoarding behaviour, they would have had a mental health counsellor present. She became increasingly agitated each time the workers loaded another bag onto the rubbish van.

The movers were very patient. In fact, this went on for days. We made sure to have someone there every day, watching the door and checking any items that might hide a kitten or two. Each night we would close as many internal doors as possible and leave fresh food and water in each, hoping that any cats in there would eat it. Then we could find them more easily. Once this was all over, we knew that there were no cats inside at all.

The only ones left were still outside, those that Si had not already managed to catch. They were three black and white longhaired cats and three black shorthaired cats. The three black and white longhaired ones had never seemed to be part of the same colony. They had rarely approached for food. We were told that one of the cats was the mother of the other two, and that a family at the opposite end of the terrace fed them and that they lived in his shed. But he had denied this.

Si kept trying to catch them, but it was clear that they were well fed. They were not interested in food.

Celia convinced me that I should go one evening so I insisted on taking Pete too.

I told Pete about Peter the cat, who was already back at the clinic, waiting for Francine to confirm that we could deliver him to her new place. Pete helped me to set up at the opposite end of the wall to my usual spot. We were much closer to the shed where the longhaired cats apparently lived. We knew of course at that at least one of these were female, and so should be the priority. If even only one female was left behind, the whole place would be overrun again quickly.

That first night, we did not manage to catch anything. None of the cats even went near the trap. But we did not see anyone or have any trouble.

We agreed to go again the next night. Pete was on his way back to me with chips for our dinner when one of the young cats jumped down from the wall and headed straight for the trap. Luckily Pete saw this in time and froze mid-step so as not to scare the cat off. I stopped where I was, poised to close the trap if the cat should go in. Instead, he wandered off to the terraces opposite, sitting on a porch step.

The lady who I had spoken to in the past about these cats came out soon after and offered us tea. We happily accepted.

When she came back out, she also brought a bowl of cat food, putting it down in her porch.

I had known she fed the cats, but she had always fed them beside the wall. She explained that she had had a confrontation with the owner and so had started feeding them on her porch instead. I explained that Francine no longer lived there. I let her leave the food down to see what would happen. She went in and closed the door and instantly five of the six remaining cats appeared from different directions and went running over. I was not going to let them eat it all, or they would be too full to be tempted by the trap. I walked over to them slowly and picked up the food, Pete replaced it with the trap. My wrists had been aching a lot recently, so I was glad of the help with lifting.

Within about fifteen minutes, we managed to catch four of the cats in the trap including the last definite female. We believed that the remaining cats were almost certainly males as they had been involved with chasing the female in season a few weeks before. We did go back a few times and managed to catch one more, but we were never able to catch that last one. After I left, months later, I gave descriptions of it to my replacement. Hopefully it has been caught by now.

A man nearby who had loved and fed the cats for years contacted us, requesting that he take some of them because he missed them. He was happy to offer them the use of his shed, which was ideal for the ferals of the group, and this also meant that they would be able to stay in a familiar place. They were all neutered and eartipped, and after they had been signed over to us officially by the council, they went to live with him. The rest were rehomed in pairs, including Peter, because despite out best efforts, we never heard from Francine again.

The Persians

I had a very confused relationship with the Persians. The negative part was not their fault of course. They had been brought into us by their owner, a woman who claimed that these 'kittens' had been left to her in a will and she had just picked them up, finding them in very poor condition. She had called first, a couple of days before, asking to bring them in when she picked them up, so she must have known at that point that they were not healthy. She had called again that morning, saying they were in a sorry state and considering cancelling the appointment because she was worried that we would judge her. I promised her 'of course we would not judge'. They had not even been in her care and we just wanted to help them. I asked her to bring them in as soon as she could, regardless of the appointment time. We would see them as an emergency if they were that bad.

There were seven of them. They were so small that they fitted into two carriers. The vets were shocked by the terrible condition that they were in. Diarrhoea was literally dripping out of them continuously, making them horribly dehydrated. The skin, when pinched, would stay in position. There was no elasticity left to it to make it go back flat (an extreme sign of dehydration). Their fur was matted into huge chunks so tight that it had torn the skin. Because of these knots, it was also difficult to see how skinny they were. But the vet said that they were emaciated.

The new owner told us they were about eight weeks old and we took her word for it at the time. It made sense when judging from the small size and slight weight of them. But later, a vet looked at their teeth and shockingly discovered that some were adults, over a year old and the others were at least four months old.

They had such a bad flu that their breathing was audible from across the room. Their eyes were so infected from the flu that they were strikingly red and watery.

They were kept isolated from the other cats because with diarrhoea so bad, who knew what diseases they might have. Samples were taken and tested. They turned out to have Corona virus, which on its own is not usually a huge problem, but it can randomly turn into FIP which will very quickly and horribly kill the cat.

The cats were initially kept loose in a room together, while we had thought that they were kittens, until we discovered some were adults. As we had not neutered them, they could very possibly impregnate each other, although it was unlikely that they were capable of it yet in their ill state. But it was not a risk worth taking. They had to be split into two pens - the boys and the girls.

It took a few days of intensive care to try to get them to gain a little weight and reduce the diarrhoea before any of the vets would even risk trying to remove the knotted fur that must have been painful for them. It was too solid to get a brush into it at all.

The knots were horrendous, and the diarrhoea had clogged into the knots, so that when they were shaved, the knots came away as large, filthy chunks of solid fur. Even, after they were shaved and cleaned and their eyes were less sore, I still could not help but think how ugly the Persian breed was with their odd squashed faces. Their skin was covered in red, sore patches, torn in some places by the tightness of the now-removed knots.

It took more weeks of a sensitive diet and antibiotics before they had the energy even to play.

As their fur grew back, I would spend my spare time sitting with them, brushing them and cuddling them. For all their ordeal, they were the sweetest, gentlest, most loving cats I had ever known. I would go to see the boys first. Charlie had red fur. He would run straight out and curl up on my lap and so he got the first brush and cuddle. Oscar was white, with bits of grey. Full of energy, he would pelt past me and run like crazy all around the room, climbing shelves then jumping off them. His fur was somehow different to the others and required a lot less brushing – luckily, because he did not like to stay still for long. I would then lean into the pen to brush Leo and Fernando, who were mottled colours. They would both cower under my touch. It was horrible, but I knew that if they were not brushed regularly, their fur would grow back into the knots and be painful again. I hoped that, with time, they would learn that I was not scary. But I worried what on earth had they gone through to be so terrified. By then I was in love with them.

It was weeks later when I opened the door and after brushing Charlie, I moved him away, about to stand to catch Oscar for his turn, Fernando ran out of the pen and jumped into my lap.

I suspected he had been wanting to do this for a while, judging by the suddenness of it. Perhaps he had been watching Charlie purr on my lap each day, wanting to trust me and get the same cuddles for himself. How could I not adore them when they were so loving? I brushed him as gently as I could and tickled him under his chin and behind his ears and scratched his head. He did not purr, but the fact that he was there at all was hugely rewarding. Of course, I could not take full credit for his trust myself. There was a small army of volunteers that were also madly in love with these cats, visiting and brushing them too. Some of them even *liked* their odd faces.

Cat Rescuer

I skipped around the building for the rest of the week, telling anyone who would listen of my cuddle with Fernando. After that first time, he wanted to be everyone's friend and became almost as cuddly as Charlie.

It took a very odd situation for a cat charity before Leo would come around too. Some rats moved into the room. There were not many rooms where there was not at least one loose cat, so they did not have much opportunity to get in. But the Persians were still in pens in their room because we still had not managed to get permission to neuter them.

When the rats arrived, as soon as the pen was opened, both Leo and Oscar would fight to get out the door first. Oscar would do his usual mad run around the room and Leo would run to the corner of the room, squash himself under the sink cupboard and watch the hole where he must have seen the rats go.

I would carry on as usual, brush Charlie, then Fernando, then give Oscar a fuss and a quick brush, then I would go and sit near Leo, and brush him gently. He ignored me touching him completely at first, so intent was he on watching the hole.

But eventually it would come time to go back in the pen. I had to lift him and put him in. I did this with great caution, with one hand on his scruff just in case he panicked. I scooped the rest of him my other arm, all the while talking softly to him and rubbing gently behind his ears. He soon got used to it. By the time the rats gave up and moved out, he was tame. He did not come for a cuddle like Charlie and Fernando, but he would wander around the room exploring, less hurriedly than Oscar, and did learn to enjoy being stroked.

Nichola Kirk

The girls were tame from the outset. One of the blue tortoiseshell girls unfortunately passed away from FIP very soon after she arrived, so I never got to know her. The names they had been given when they arrived were all confused as they did not match the cats that had been brought in properly. We think that she was called 'Venice'.

Katya was a blue tortoiseshell. She was a lot like Oscar and liked to do her own thing and explore. She was even crazier though and would climb everything and anything. She would frustratingly urinate on the computer keyboard in the room, and climb the shelves pulling down all the folders. I let her get away with anything, just picking up her mess after her, like any good cat servant. She was the hardest to keep brushed because she was constantly on the move. I would follow her brushing her while she walked. She would occasionally turn and nip me gently to tell me to leave her alone.

My favourite of all the Persians was Bridget, she had red fur, slightly darker than Charlie's.

Bridget was the most beautiful Persian. Her nose was less squished than the others and she had the longest soft fur when it grew back fully. She would purr and press herself against me when I picked her up as though she was cuddling me back. I think the main reason she was my favourite was that she was so much more vulnerable. She was the tiniest of the six and I felt very protective of her. She put on weight more slowly than the others. Although she eventually made it to a relatively healthy weight, she stayed small. She also seemed to get matted the quickest. I spent the longest time of every visit to the Persians with Bridget — brushing her, cuddling her, loving her. She was the gentlest cat I knew during my time at the charity. So graceful and delicate. I had bad wrists at the time, I thought it must be repetitive strain injury from overuse carrying heavy baskets all the time, but it did not stop me from brushing her.

The cats eventually got to a stage where intensive care was no longer necessary. Celia and the vets invited their owner in for a chat about the care they would need when they went home. Celia wanted to discuss whether she planned to get them neutered and explain why we were such advocates of this. Most importantly, we wanted to be absolutely sure that we were not sending them back to the same person who had let them get into such a state in the first place. The woman appeared to care very much about them and gave details of her own black shorthaired cat who looked very healthy, judging by the photo that she showed us. She said she would send us details of the will in which she had inherited the cats. All seemed well, so we made plans for their return in the near future.

The Will documents never materialised. We asked if she had anything at all that could show that she did not already own them at the time that they had been so severely neglected. That was when she became aggressive and started making threats. Soon after, she swore at Wendy over the phone. She said she was going to find out where Wendy lived, threatening to get a friend to bring a truckload of farm manure to dump on her driveway. Our receptionist was really shaken up.

Celia wrote to the owner asking her to please liaise with us only in writing and to not come into the clinic as we could not tolerate that kind of behaviour toward the staff who worked so hard.

She got a solicitor involved and we corresponded through him, asking again for the same evidence that had already been promised that would show that the cats had been in someone else's care at the time of their neglect.

We just could not understand why she had not provided this yet, she had promised it before.

It soon became clear when her solicitor forwarded us the receipts for the cats — for some reason thinking that he needed to prove her ownership of them. We initially thought that perhaps she had bought them just before bringing them to us, not inherited them. But the receipts showed that she had actually purchased the cats months before, proving without a doubt that she had owned them at the time of their neglect.

We passed this evidence on to the RSPCA, asking them to investigate. They accepted the case and went to meet the owner in her multiple homes. They advised us that there was no reason to not give the cats back. Except, we thought, the condition that the cats had gotten into whilst in her care.

Soon after all of this, another of the cats deteriorated in just one day from lively and happy in the morning, to desperately ill in the evening. It was Bridget. My sweet little baby girl. She looked so pale and weak. I helped one of the nurses change her bedding. She could hardly move. I lifted her easily — she was so light — and held her while the nurse changed her bed. She laid limp in my arms. She had no energy to even look up at me. I cuddled her to me and whispered to her that it would be ok, that the nurses would help her and she would be better soon.

But it was not going to be ok. She died that night.

It still hurts so much to know that despite all our efforts, it still was not enough to get her over the earlier neglect.

Then their owner tried to sue the charity for return of them. How dare she? How dare she own her multiple houses and fancy cars and pay no attention whatsoever while her cats almost died around her? How dare she pretend to love them and demand them back when she knew she was responsible for Venice and Bridget's death?

Cat Rescuer

The RSPCA refused to help any further. So Celia and I stayed up late every night for weeks. Neither of us knew much about law, but we put together our counter case.

I had recently hurt my feet — I had thought from wearing bad shoes — and so was limping and struggling to drive. My ankles and knees had started to hurt too. So the excuse to do more office work was welcome.

Now that we had the receipts of the cats sale, our case for not giving back the cats was simple. We contacted the previous owners and they confirmed when they had sold the owner the cats. They were all so helpful in sending us pictures of them as kittens. Bridget as a kitten was adorable. It was upsetting to see the photo. She had looked such a healthy bundle of fluff. She had looked so gentle even then. We checked the markings against our pictures of her, checking the position of the little bit of white on each of her toes, to be sure that it was definitely the same cat. It was, without a doubt.

Another prior owner also sent us pictures of two others, and we were able to confirm the same with these too. We contacted a Persian expert who studied the images and the receipts and were able to confirm that at least these three were definitely the same. We concluded that these three at least must have been in her care when they were neglected.

The owner had sent in receipts for seven cats, as we had been brought in seven cats. At least two of the receipts were for cats that did not match the cats that we had at the clinic. We had not realised this ourselves. We are not Persian experts and the colours had seemed about right, but after consulting an expert, we were told that the breed types were wrong. This showed she must have owned at least two more cats, that we had never seen, and that the RSPCA had not been shown when visiting her. What state of neglect were they in? Were they still alive? Perhaps they had died already and that was why she had not brought them in. If so, she had not been paying attention to which had survived and which she had brought into us.

Perhaps she had a shed somewhere where she bred cats and kept her cruelty hidden? A couple of the people she bought kittens from told us that she had openly identified herself to them as a breeder. We managed to find her on a pet sale website selling two kittens of a different breed. They did not look in great condition either, judging from the flu discharge in their eyes. But they appeared to be in a clean home.

Perhaps she brought them out for photos of wherever she bred them. Just like the puppy farmers do. No puppy from a puppy farm is sold directly from the shed that they are born in. They are cleaned and bathed first and shown off to new potential buyers in the house. No one would buy them if they saw them in the state they are kept in.

The RSPCA again were unable to help us investigate this. We tried but failed to find them ourselves. All C.H.A.T could do was protect the surviving five from her, by any means necessary.

The court case was repeatedly adjourned. She never gave a good impression to the judge, which worked in our favour. The judge was very helpful in telling us what we needed to provide at the next session. The owner's solicitor did not seem to understand our main argument – that we had a legal obligation to ensure that we protected these animals from harm. We asked only for evidence that they had not been in her care at the time of neglect. Whereupon she had provided the evidence to the contrary. So we were now legally obliged to ensure their safety by not returning them to her.

The fear was that, as she had proved ownership of the cats, the court would insist that the charity give them back to her.

The court had asked us to tell them the worth of the cats. We proved that they were not worth anything monetarily at all, because they were too contagious and delicate to be sold for breeding and, considering the ongoing treatment that they may need for the rest of their lives, no one would pay money for them as a pet. Celia worried that the court would decide to imprison her for the theft of the cats, if she still insisted that she would not return them.

In court, it was clear that the owner was not doing herself any favours. She soon realised that it was not going well for her. The charity considered going public to find a lawyer. The owner said she would drop the case and the charity could keep the cats, with each paying their own fees only if they did not report her name publicly. Celia was reluctant because she wanted to protect future cats from being bought by the owner. But she was so worried about the possibility of jail and the rising cost of the case that she eventually agreed to it. The Persians were rehomed in secret via people that Celia already knew who liked Persians, to ensure they would not end up in the wrong hands again.

Cemetery 2

The second time I had to spend much of the night in a cemetery was right at the end of my time at the charity. This time it was in a churchyard in Dagenham. Celia had been there the night before, advised of a situation by one of our regular, friendly cat ladies. She had been informed of a colony where all but one female had been neutered. It does not matter if you have neutered all the males in a colony, as other males will travel miles. An unneutered female will still get pregnant. This particular female was now trap-shy - the cat ladies had used an automatic trap. She was currently on her fourth litter since they had started monitoring the colony. Most of the kittens had been caught and rehomed or neutered and returned. Her current litter were only a few days old.

Celia wanted to be prepared so between the two of us, we carried a manual trap, a queen cage, a standard carrier, some chicken, sardines, tins of various types of food, kitten food pouches, four thick blankets (some for ourselves as well as the cats — it was a really cold night), three torches, extra batteries, and a waterproofed box cut to create a cat bed.

Normally in this situation we would see how close we could get to the mother, approaching slowly and cautiously and offering food ahead of us to see if she was tame enough to let us get hold of her. If the cat was not tame, once we got close enough that she looked as though she was going to run, we would approach faster, so that she would panic and run quickly. If we gave mother cats time to think about it, they may pick up a kitten and run with it to hide it. Once the mother cat was out of the way, we would be able to put the kittens in a carrier towards the back of a trap to help us catch the mother. However, we had been told that the cat ladies had tried this before with this particular mother cat. She had refused to go in the trap to her kittens, and they had ended up having to hand-rear them.

This cat was tucked into a slight dent in the ground, behind a tree, by the cemetery wall.

Celia approached carefully but the cat did not run. Celia reached for her, but she lashed out violently. Celia made a few more attempts to get close but soon backed away, her hand dripping with blood.

She was so worried about the cat that she barely noticed the blood. I passed her a tissue and she covered the cuts, then got out more chicken and tried again, whispering soothingly to the mother cat. The cat hissed and spat and swiped out her front paws at Celia. Celia had to cover her arm with her coat and a blanket, and even that was barely enough protection.

The cat was well-positioned behind the tree at an angle that made it difficult for us to be able to get to her scruff. Celia got so close so many times that it was almost impossible to want to leave, surely she would get her at the next attempt.

It had been dark when we arrived, but as it got later, it got spookier. The grass was overgrown, and I kept hearing noises behind us and spinning around in fear. It was probably a cat or a fox, but I could not see far through the dark and the tall grass. Celia was probably starting to get annoyed with my being so jumpy and distracting her. But then there was another noise, from behind the wall. It sounded much bigger than a cat or a fox. We both looked at each other, listening, wondering, worrying.

Suddenly a shape appeared above us. We both jumped with surprise…

… it was just a person.

Nichola Kirk

The man had come to find out what we were up to in a graveyard at midnight. And to tell us off for shining our torches into their flat window. We explained what we were doing and apologised for the torches, promising to keep them pointed down. He left us alone in the dark again.

After another attempt at trying to scruff the cat, she jumped up and ran off. She only had one little kitten in her nest. No wonder she was so protective if she only had one left, after all her previous babies had been taken away from her.

It cried at first for her, but soon curled up in the leaves and went back to sleep. We waited for the mother to come back for a while. She did stay nearby, watching us from further down the wall. But after we had waited for at least another hour, we realised that she was not going to come back while we were there, so we left her a bowl of tasty food. We would go back tomorrow.

We were then faced with the dilemma of whether to take the kitten with us or not.

If we took the kitten, she would have no reason to stick around long enough to give us a chance of getting a hand on her. This might be her only chance to get neutered, rather than giving birth to endless litters of kittens born under trees in a cemetery.

If we left the kitten, there was a good chance she might move it. If she did, we might not find it again until it was walking and came out from hiding when it was much older. But if we did not leave it, we would not be able to catch her. We decided to leave it there. At least if she did move it, it was only one to catch later. In the meantime, we would have time to try using dummy traps to get her acclimatised with them before she became pregnant again.

I set up the box-bed under some bushes a few feet away, just in case she did decide to move the kitten, giving her an option that would be more advantageous for us.

Cat Rescuer

Back at the clinic everyone except Pete had already left. I went straight to bed to try to recover from the very long day. Celia did not go to bed. She never did until the morning, usually between 3-5am. Sometimes she would not go to bed at all. She would stay up catching up on her emails. The charity received a lot and she dealt with all of the Canning Town clinic's emails personally. Or she would watch cute cat videos all night, while cuddling an ill cat, kitten or puppy. Si would often turn up at 6am, grab his equipment and tell her to go to bed. Then he would go out trapping. He would come back three hours later to find her still there in the same spot, doing the same thing. Or fast asleep in her chair, with all the staff tiptoeing around her, trying to let her get some sleep before the next crisis.

The next morning I was exhausted. My wrists ached so much that I could barely lift one empty basket. I tried to take it easy. I got help with carrying wherever possible and parked at the front of the clinic to drop off cats rather than the back.

That evening, once the clinic was closed, and Celia finally managed to get free, we headed back to the cemetery.

I tried to bring only what we were likely to need. But Celia insisted that we would be taking everything again 'just in case'. I explained about my aching wrists and that most of what we had taken the night before had not been necessary, and she said that she would carry some so I would be ok.

As we arrived, Celia rushed ahead. By the time I caught up, Celia was already lying on the ground, offering the cat some hot chicken. The cat was hissing and spitting at her angrily. She made a move closer, and the cat jumped up and ran. She clearly was not in the mood this time. Celia checked the hole, but the kitten was gone.

We checked a few places but could not find where she had moved it to.

There was nothing more we could do that night.

The next morning, I contacted the original one-woman rescue organisation that had caught and neutered the rest of the colony. She told me the whole story of how they had used automatic traps to catch the whole colony successfully — apart from this one female. I told her of my plan to tie up a dummy trap with a bicycle lock (so it would not be picked up as scrap) to a tree near where the cat was usually fed. I asked her to contact anyone who fed the cats to please feed only beside the dummy trap for a few weeks. She agreed to do this on the condition that the mother would be returned to the colony and not rehomed. I agreed this was the best option. The mother would be much happier there anyway.

I tried to check back with her but was surprised when she did not return my calls, and the cat ladies would not answer the phone to me. I found out from some other cat ladies that the cats were fed in the morning.

Si agreed to go one morning. He was able to confirm that most of the cats were eartipped.

There were a few however that were not eartipped, so he caught them, just in case. But all of them were male. We neutered them and returned them all a week later.

Si eventually managed to meet one of the feeders. She let him know that the cat was still around. She explained that they were not feeding in the dummy trap because the other rescue organisation had asked them not to, because they did not believe that we would return the cat, despite my assurances. It turned out that Celia had worked with this charity before and had rehomed a cat that they thought should have been neutered and returned. There had been a falling out over it.

Si explained that we had every intention of bringing this cat back. But also that we were determined to get her neutered for her own good. I had never heard of a cat having just one and so we could only assume that something bad must have happened to the rest. Surely this could not be allowed to repeat. The feeder agreed with Si and said she would feed in the dummy trap from now on. But she never did, and by the time I left the charity, we still had not managed to catch that one last cat. Perhaps we could have with the other charity's help.

In the end

One morning I woke up and realised that my feet, my ankles, my knees and my wrists were all hurting at the same time. I had put my feet down to bad shoes and my wrists to carrying heavy trapping equipment around all day. But now I suspected there might be something else wrong. My mum had Rheumatoid Arthritis: which is supposedly not hereditary. But these pains did all seem to be in my joints and were much worse than I would have expected had they really been caused by bad shoes and overworking. My doctor took some blood to send away. He did not say what he thought it might be. I still left in tears, calling my partner trying to explain how afraid I was that I might have the same awful, incurable, degenerative condition as my mum and his mum too.

Around the same time, a at rescue situation also led to breaking me emotionally. It was a Wednesday in Spring. Light grey sky with hopes that the sun would push through the clouds soon. I started off the day with a quick, easy trapping job. I forget now where the cat came from, that was not the important thing about her. She was just an average, black, feral. Just like many others that I caught all the time. The trapping of her was not memorable or different in any way to all the other feral cats that I had caught.

After dropping her off, I went out to take some kittens to a foster home. I loved my time visiting the fosterers, I always got to play with the kittens and I enjoyed discussing their developing personalities.

When I got back to the clinic for lunch, someone had just dropped off a kitten in a carrier that they had found in a nearby park. Two kittens had been dumped in the carrier, but the other had escaped. Si had gone straight out to the park and was looking for the other kitten already.

Cat Rescuer

I left him to it whilst I picked up an owned limping cat from a disabled lady in Stratford and dropped it off at the clinic for a check-up.

Si had to head off home. He had looked everywhere for the kitten in the park and put a notice up asking anyone who found it to let us know. He had left tactical piles of food and had asked everyone he saw if they had seen it but no one had.

I arranged with him that I would go later that day and check the piles of food.

We informed Celia of our arrangement, but she wanted me to go there and then. I told her that I had to induct a new volunteer and then drop the owned cat back off home and then would go to the park.

Celia was worried about the poor kitten in the park, despite the futility of going so soon after Si had searched. It must have found somewhere good to hide and was unlikely to come out again whilst the park was busy.

Where most people accept that you can only do what you can do, Celia would rather try to move Heaven and Earth. Celia decided that she would go to the park herself.

Two hours later, I called Celia, who had gotten held up at the clinic and had not made it to the park. So I went and had a good look around. I called Si, who directed me to where he had left the piles of food. All of these were untouched. I sat by a tree quietly to watch and wait. Celia called and I explained that I had been at the park a while and had not seen or heard anything. I told her that all was very quiet and no people had passed through the park at all since I had been there. I put up some more posters further along, and around the corners.

I then went to drop off some food at a foster home before it was too late to do so.

When I got back to the clinic, I could not find anyone. After looking everywhere, I called Celia. The conversation went something like this:

'Where are you?'

'I'm at the park with Pete.'

'I've already been to the park'

'I know but I wanted to check too. How did you get in to the park?'

'Through the black gate nearest the main road'

'How?'

'What do you mean 'how'?'

'It's locked.'

'Oh. Well, it wasn't when I was there.'

'Did you climb it?'

'No, it was unlocked.'

'I'm going to climb it. Pete, stand there and let me stand on your knee.'

I could hear scuffling noises through the phone.

'I can't get in. We're going to have to walk around the outside and see what we can see from here.'

I asked, 'Do you know that there are still cats to be put away here?'

Celia responded, 'Yes Nichola, but I can't do everything at once can I?'

In my head I was thinking that she really did not need to have gone to the park at all, Si and I would do everything possible to find the cat and that she would be much better off at the clinic deciding where to put these cats. I realised that it would not help to say this out loud.

I responded, 'I just thought you might have put them away before you went out. Where do you want me to put them?'

'I couldn't think of anywhere. We'll figure it out when I get back'

'Can I put one in the hospital basket from where the cat went home earlier, and another one in with the others upstairs? I have a spare pen in my van that I picked up from a foster home that I could use for the last one for now.'

'Fine, Pete can help later.'

'Ok, thanks. Good luck finding the kitten. See you later.'

I disinfected all the pens I intended to use and decided to put the feral black cat away first as she had been waiting since that morning. She was supposed to have been neutered in the day, but it looked as though they had been too busy. She had been in the ward all day, but at least she had been fed.

She was going in a feral hospital basket in the Rescue office temporarily. Due to the building work at the back of the clinic, to get her there I would have to take her outside and around the whole building to get to the rescue office at the back.

I moved her back into a carrier and put her in a trolley that we used to carry heavy things around from the storage in the other building. I covered her over to help keep her calm.

As I got to the gate at the back, I heard the oddest mew from her. She sounded like a kitten. Poor thing. I felt guilty for stressing her and started to hurry. I opened the gate and pulled the trolley into the yard. Just as I was locking the gate, I heard another mew. There was something strange about it. A bit too kitten-like a mew for her size. I lifted a corner of the blanket to find a pair of terrified yellow eyes, wide and staring, and a tiny, wet, newborn kitten struggling to climb up the owner of those eyes.

'Oh my goodness! She's giving birth!' I exclaimed, talking to myself, 'What do I do?!'

No one had realised she was pregnant.

I had been at the charity for three years. I had brought to life puppies born by caesarean section. I had hand-fed newborn kittens. I had fostered hundreds of kittens from birth. But I had never, ever, seen a cat give birth.

Under normal circumstances the cat would have been giving birth in a space she had chosen herself. She would be relatively calm and would deal with it herself quite competently, ideally safely in a foster home.

But these were not normal circumstances. She was locked in a wire cat carrier, outside, with barely enough room to move. As I watched, the kitten's feet almost fell through the wire bottom of the cage where the blanket had lifted slightly.

I broke into a full blown, hysterical, brain explosion panic attack. Breathlessly I put my hand under the carrier, nudging the newborn kitten on top of the blanket. Tears started falling down my cheeks. This was very unlike me. Normally I would deal with the situation at hand and cry later. I had felt the tension building all day, partly with the amount of work I had to get through, and partly with the whole world for doing ridiculous things like dumping kittens in parks beside busy roads. Even more likely, this was a result of the strain that had been building since I had started such a fast-paced, emotional job, not to mention the imminent diagnosis of my joint condition.

I forced myself into crisis mode. I could not take the cat into the rescue building now. There was flu in the next room and I could not risk putting newborn kittens anywhere near that. An adult could have recovered easily from flu but it could kill the kittens.

I would have to take the cat back to the main clinic and work out what to do with her from there. I grabbed an extra blanket that I'd brought round on top of the basket and stuffed it under the whole cage so that if the kitten did end up at the bottom again, at least it could not fall through the bars. It was so tiny still mewing and trying to climb it's mum who was completely ignoring it.

I hurried back as quickly as I could, trying to pull the trolley smoothly around any bumps in the road. I called Celia in the process for advice. I told her what was happening and her response was 'Oh no… where are we going to put her?' She had no suggestions though as the clinic was overwhelmingly full.

I set up a bed in the hospital basket I'd already earmarked for her with a thick, clean blanket. I covered most of the basket with a donated bedsheet doubled over to give her a dark, safe space. She was much too cramped in the carrier to be able to give birth comfortably. I would have to run her into the basket as she was too feral to lift in. Normally, I would just put the two baskets end to end and lift the dividers between them, with the dark space furthest away from me, letting her run across. I could not do this though because the cat had not yet bitten the kitten's umbilical cord – the kitten was still attached to her.

I split the pen with a divider in half and ran her in half-way, then moved the kitten up next to her, before letting her go into the other half. She curled herself up tightly at the other end on the blanket and I pushed the kitten up next to her. She struck out at my hand which started to pour with blood, so I quickly wrapped a tissue round it and made sure the kitten could reach its mum to get itself to milk and then called the vet nurse to ask what to do about the cord.

By now I was crying hysterically and the nurse had difficulty getting out of me what I actually needed from him. He managed to calm me a little and explain that it was ok, cats give birth every day and she would be fine. He could come, if needed, within minutes, but that I did not need to panic.

He told me where to get the sterile blades to cut it with, and the clamps so it would not bleed. I looked through all the drawers in the surgery and there were none. I tried the other surgery and still could not find them. I went back to the first room, looking more carefully and there they were in a drawer I had already looked in. I had to get the kitten out but had to very careful about how I opened the door. My head filled with images of the cat running around the large waiting room, wild and terrified, dragging her baby's body behind her. I have never been so careful in my life to make sure I did not leave an inch available for her to escape through.

I put my hand under the door and moved to pick up the kitten. The mother attacked me again. I should have expected that really. My hand was bleeding more, but it was not important right then. I hid my hand under a folded towel and manoeuvred, with the phone tucked against my shoulder on one ear, while holding the basket lid tightly down and listened while the nurse told me where to put the clamps and then how to cut through the cord. It was tougher than it looked and took me a few seconds to get through even with a sharp blade.

It did not look as though the cat had washed the kitten yet as it was still wet with amniotic fluid. I brought the kitten out of the basket once it was no longer attached and gave it a thorough rub in the towel.

Once it was looking a bit drier, fluffier and wrigglier, I put it back in with the mother.

As I was tucking it up next to her to feed (with my hand protected with the towel in case she attacked again) I noticed the cat had just given birth again. Only this time, the kitten was still in the fluid-filled amniotic sac.

She was clearly too terrified to do anything about it as she stared at me with wide eyes, her body tense. She had been through so much already that day.

Thankfully I still had the calm, experienced nurse waiting on the phone. I made a sort of hysterical shriek at him before telling him another kitten had arrived.

He told me exactly what to do, I cut open the sack, very carefully, to find the kitten inside. Then I clamped and cut the umbilical cord. I wrapped the kitten in a towel, and brought it out of the cage, rubbing it in the towel. I had to rub hard enough to encourage it to breathe, while softly enough to protect its miniature limp body.

As I rubbed, it made a little squeak, shortly followed by more squeaks as it awakened.

I let the nurse go, with a promise to call him immediately if anything went wrong.

I rubbed the kitten until it was mewing normally and was dry enough to not get cold. Then I covered my hand again with a towel and tucked the second kitten up to its mother. The first was struggling to find a nipple to feed from because the cat was still curled up so tightly. I tried to encourage her to lay out a little better by pulling at her blanket a little, and managed to make enough room for both kittens to get in.

I moved the whole basket into a quiet corner of the waiting room and covered her over with another sheet to make it darker for her, in the hope she would feel somewhat secure. I fetched her a big bowl of chicken and a bowl of water. When I got back, both kittens had latched on and were feeding happily.

I then left the room to give her time and space, and to try to get myself back into some sort of sensible state.

As much as I wanted to sit by her and be there for her, as I might have with any owned cat, I knew that this would be the worst thing I could do for this one. Especially as I was probably sending out stress hormones myself too. The sight of her wide, yellow eyes still haunts me.

I paced for a while, trying to focus, to stop myself shaking from the adrenalin and emotional overload. But the anger, the frustration, the pain and guilt kept all rolling over me in waves. I feared that this was it — the breaking point for me.

It was a sense of something indescribable, almost like grief, a crushing weight of failure that I knew could push me over the edge. I had suggested before that I wanted to leave the charity as it was too much, emotionally, but I had never meant it. Yet now I knew with a certainty that I could no longer stay. I had to get out before I really did break.

I am not sure quite how exactly the horror that I felt about that poor cat caused such extreme feelings in me, especially after everything else that I had seen, experienced and coped with. But even now I associate that specific cat with my reasons for leaving C.H.A.T. All these years I had been wondering, 'Why am I doing this to myself? Why am I working all these hours and exhausting myself to such an extreme day after day? Why am I suffering along with every cat I pick up as I feel its pain?' Of course, I knew why – for them.

But I had not done this cat any favours. I had made its life hell. Perhaps the guilt was just too much to bear. It would have been better off not having been caught, at least in the short-term. Would the guilt of doing nothing to help them be any worse? It was a risk I had not been prepared to take before. But now it was time to go. In the past, whenever anyone had suggested I should leave, I always answered, 'No, I'm not done yet, I can still help'.

Perhaps the reason I left was because I had hit a brick wall with how much more I could improve the charity. I had repeatedly laid out my plans for the only way that I could perceive that we could win the war against cat breeding. There were certain necessary improvements and adjustments that the charity would have to make. It would have to set up one new operating theatre dedicated to the neutering of feral cats, with its own full-time vet. It would need a room dedicated to neuter and return cats only (which it has since done). How else could we realistically make a dent in helping the 1,000,000 strays of London? How could I go on rescuing cats when I knew that I was doomed to fail in my overall objective?

I also had the physical pain to deal with. My joints had not improved. By the time I left the charity, I had just been diagnosed with Rheumatoid Arthritis. I knew I would not be able to keep up such physical work.

I discussed all of this with Celia after a few days of making sure that I was sure about leaving and she said she did not want to lose me. She offered for Pete to come out with me to help in the short term to help and to renew efforts to get another Rescue Worker to help in the day. This was very helpful with my physical issues but could not help with my emotional exhaustion. I ended up training the new Rescue Worker when she arrived to be my replacement rather than my assistant.

I am still of the same opinion — that I was doomed to fail. I could have carried on helping individual cats, but my ambitions were too high to settle for that. I still hold out some sense of hope that perhaps this book will reach enough people, and that it will spell out more clearly than anyone has ever shown before how truly desperate the stray cat situation is in this country.

And perhaps it might just make you re-think letting your cat have 'just one litter' or dumping your cat on a shelter's doorstep because you are struggling right now, even though you know your situation will get better soon. Or maybe you will make the extra effort to get your kitten neutered at four months before you let it out of the house so as not to 'accidentally' contribute to a crisis that is already out of control.

None of these things are bad things. You are not a bad person if you have done any of these things. Cruelty is not the hardest part of Animal Rescue. The hardest part is knowing that in a nation of animal lovers, where almost everyone has a pet, there are too many who just do not know how bad it really is and contribute unsuspectingly.

If you think you would you do any of these things again, go volunteer just one day a week in an animal shelter for a few months and then you will see what I mean.

You will meet the animals living in cages. You will meet the sweetest old-lady-cat who nobody adopts for a whole year. You will argue with the staff over the two cats that do not get along but are living in a cage together, and be offered the opportunity to separate them if only you can find where to move one of them to, then fail to find anywhere better, because there is nowhere.

In summer, you will see a litter of kittens getting bigger and bigger each week — until they are adult cats and still in the shelter — not because nobody wants them, but simply because there are so many more kittens than homes in the summer. You will stroke the tame cat who ended up there through no fault of his own, who grew up loved, and knows what it is like to be loved, as he rubs himself against the bars of his cage, then purrs in your ear and kisses your cheek, only for you to realise you have two hundred more cats to feed and clean and love, and so you only have time to cuddle him for five minutes… or maybe just five more.

Epilogue

On the day that I left C.H.A.T I adopted a Yorkie cross called Frankie. He used to chase cyclists and try to bite postmen. I have managed to train most of his bad habits out of him, apart from the barking. But I cannot stop that – he loves barking too much. I married the same man that I lived with at C.H.A.T, who supported me through everything in a gorgeous ceremony up North, near my parent's home. We had our first child in 2015. We adopted two cats that were being given away by a member of our family who could not look after them due to moving to a city-centre rented accommodation. My arthritis is well-managed by medication and I sometimes feel like I could still work at C.H.A.T but then I try to open a jar of pasta sauce and realise I could never carry multiple cats in a basket. Or I will be playing hide and seek with my daughter and realise I am physically unable to crouch on my tiptoes without horrible pain, when I used to spend hours crouching, waiting. I have fond memories of the charity and felt like my head was exploding with stories, which was why my husband bought me this laptop (thank you!) and I have written them down for your enjoyment. Sometimes those memories come with a sense of grief because I wish desperately that I could have finished the mission that I set myself of saving every cat in London, but it was not meant to be. I am so in awe of Celia that she keeps going, and everyone that stills works there. I hope these stories teach some people too about the desperate plight of London cats and so more people take steps to help them. If enough people become aware, then maybe, collectively, we really can finally make a difference to the lives of the stray cats of London. I can hope.

Printed in Great Britain
by Amazon